TAROT *by the* MOON

About the Author

Victoria Constantino is a longtime tarot practitioner and seeker of visionary wisdom. She spent more than a decade as an editor and publisher of literary fiction and nonfiction, and was the managing editor for a prominent women's lifestyle magazine. She left the field of publishing to focus on her writing and spiritual practice. Her previous publications include poetry and fiction, and instructional guides for a business publisher. She attended the University of Oxford and holds a master's degree in writing.

Tarot by the Moon

by the

Moon

XVIII

THE MOON

Spreads & Spells for Every Month of the Year

Victoria Constantino

Llewellyn Publications · Woodbury, Minnesota

FIRST EDITION
Third Printing, 2022

Cover design by Kevin R. Brown
Editing by Marjorie Otto
Interior art by Llewellyn Art Department, based on drawings by the author except for pages 56, 79, 93, 97, 105, 168, and 214.

Llewellyn is a registered trademark of Llewellyn Worldwide Ltd.

Library of Congress Cataloging-in-Publication Data
Names: Constantino, Victoria, author.
Title: Tarot by the moon : spreads & spells for every month of the year / Victoria Constantino.
Description: First edition. | Woodbury, MN : Llewellyn Publications, [2021] | Includes bibliographical references and index. | Summary: "Use the power of the moon to manifest change through tarot spreads, spells, and rituals"-- Provided by publisher.
Identifiers: LCCN 2021029192 (print) | LCCN 2021029193 (ebook) | ISBN 9780738767123 (paperback) | ISBN 9780738767185 (ebook)
Subjects: LCSH: Tarot. | Moon--Miscellanea.
Classification: LCC BF1879.T2 .C66 2021 (print) | LCC BF1879.T2 (ebook) | DDC 133.3/2424--dc23
LC record available at https://lccn.loc.gov/2021029192
LC ebook record available at https://lccn.loc.gov/2021029193

Llewellyn Publications
A Division of Llewellyn Worldwide Ltd.
2143 Wooddale Drive
Woodbury, MN 55125-2989
www.llewellyn.com

Printed in the United States of America

Dedication

This book is for the seekers, for the change-makers,
for those who endeavor to understand the universe in which they find themselves.

Acknowledgments

I would first and foremost like to acknowledge my support team in the nonphysical for guiding me into making this book a reality, and for their constant presence, guidance, and communication with me throughout its development. My sincere gratitude to my editors, Barbara Moore and Marjorie Otto, and to everyone at Llewellyn who connected with my vision and nurtured it into physical form.

I cannot overstate the gratitude I feel to live in a time and a society in which I can express the words contained herein without negative repercussion. Looking back in history, it is no small thing to be able to write and express these ideas freely, and although it is an essential freedom, it is also an honor I do not take lightly. In the writing of this book, I have remained keenly aware of those who came before me—the seekers, the mystics, the dreamers, the visionaries—and their contributions to our understanding, whether those were published, written in secret and given over to time, or simply wondered at in flickering moments then absorbed into the collective consciousness.

I am profoundly grateful to the readers of this book. It is my sincere desire that it guides you on your path to understanding, and that your quest for knowledge is lifelong. I hope you always strive to see beyond the veil.

Contents

INTRODUCTION

The moon is engaged in a perpetual dance with the earth. The powerful lunar energy affects our thinking and behavior, and the cycles and rhythms in which we live our lives. It affects the mammals and birds and the fish of the sea. The moon is an undeniable force, the energy of the Goddess writ large across the sky. It is a source of intrigue uniting untold spans of time and countless generations.

Is it any wonder we are so enthralled by the moon, that we find it so enchanting, so impossible to resist its pull? More than half of our physical composition is water. The moon's gravity affects us as it affects the tides, and perhaps even more so. On a full moon night, more babies are born and more crimes of passion committed. The tides can only advance and recede, but we can create or destroy, curse or cure.

It's no surprise we name the full moons in language as mesmeric and various as the shifting phases of the moon itself. Because much of this lunar nomenclature derives from Native American tribes, who created a system to mark the characteristics of certain time periods, there are nearly as many variations in full moon names as there were people to name them. Many tribes used the moon as a system for tracking times and seasons, and different groups sometimes used the same name for moons in separate months. For those reasons, you will sometimes find crossover and duplication in the names among different sources. Other moon names hail from old lore and early North American settlers. With so many traditions contributing to the naming, this book strives to include the most commonly used full moon names.

It is from a place of fascination, both with the ancient lore and with the moon itself, that I have written this book. One of my earliest memories is reaching toward the moon, my arms stretching upward as high as they would go. "I want to kiss the moon!" was my fervent plea, and then, I truly believed it was possible, if my mother would just hold me up a little bit higher. Now, I know that humankind's ages-old love for the moon has created a collective love and admiration around that planetary body, which it reflects back to us. We don't have to physically touch the moon; we are already connected to its energy.

As a lifelong seeker and natural witch, I have always connected with the earth and with the moon, which is a force of nature, of the cosmos, a body created and held by universal energies. Some of the spells in this book are from my own personal repertoire and I have crafted all of them in concert with my higher guidance. Much of this book is channeled. It is designed to bring healing to all who read it, to assist you on the paths of awareness and manifestation, and to help bridge a stronger connection with your inner being or higher self, between you and the greater aspect of you, and with your own intuition.

Tarot and the Moon

Human beings have been attempting to peer beyond the veil since time immemorial. Foretelling one's future through cards, or *cartomancy,* is one of many methods of divination. Divination itself is defined in Merriam-Webster as "the art or practice that seeks to foresee or foretell future events or discover hidden knowledge, usually by the interpretation of omens or by the aid of supernatural powers and alternately, as "unusual insight" and "intuitive perception." That is the dictionary definition. A further look reveals the word *divine* implied in the prefix *divin-,* which comes from the Latin *divinus,* meaning "of a god"; in the suffix *-ation* implies the bringing forth (*-ation* indicates the product or result of action); therefore, the word, at its essence, means "to bring forth the divine." Who better than the all-seeing, all-knowing, all-powerful divine to connect with in our asking of what the future may bring?

Whether you use the tarot with the intention of tapping into the divine, connecting with your own divinity, working with guides, angels, and high-vibrational allies, or if your goals are to provide guidance for practical, everyday questions and to further your own self-knowledge and growth, there is something in tarot for everyone.

Appreciators of cartomancy might argue it is one of the most beloved of all divination methods for its incisive pictorial history, which is distilled into archetypal renderings of the human experience. The oldest decks we are currently aware of date from the fifteenth century, but it's only in the last few hundred years that it has gained traction in common use. The twenty-first century has seen a dramatic upsurge in the number of new tarot and oracle decks, coinciding with tarot's rise in popularity. While the tarot is a type of oracle, which is simply a means of predicting the future, oracle cards are structured differently, as they are typically not beholden to suits and not separated into the major and minor arcana.

Divination itself is classed into four categories—pattern divination, trance divination, omen divination, and symbol divination; tarot finds its place in the latter category. *Pattern divination* is sometimes defined as a means of producing patterns in an artificial way to determine the outcome of future events, such as reading coffee grounds or interpreting the shapes of wax poured into water. However, the interpretation of patterns does not have to be artificially derived. Gazing at the leaves in a tree or the arrangement of stones on the ground to spot patterns of significance is a natural means of pattern divination. *Trance divination* infers what is to come through messages received through the physical senses in a trance or dream state. *Omen divination* is based on the idea that naturally occurring signs, such as a sudden peal of thunder or planetary alignments, have some bearing on what is to come or offer information about the state of things. *Symbol divination* uses a fixed system to analyze the outcome of a situation or provide information about a specific question. Because the *I Ching*, a Chinese divination text, and tarot are based on fixed symbols, they fall under the umbrella of symbol divination.

Among the many methods of divination are *tasseography*, or the reading of tea leaves (sometimes also referred to as *tassomancy* or *tasseomancy*; see chapter 7 for a ritual involving this practice), palm reading or palmistry, the use of runes and pendulums, scrying with water and black mirrors, and numerology, to name but a few. What they all have in common is the use of intuition as an interpretive method. Tapping into the intuition is more art than science, and is rewarded by practice. Like a muscle, the more you put it to use, the stronger it becomes. Ways to connect with and strengthen your intuition are interspersed throughout this book.

That being said, you don't have to be psychic to be a good tarot reader or have a direct channel to the divine (although it certainly doesn't hurt). Of primary importance is the energy with which you approach a reading. In other words, when you are open to receiving the messages that come through, whether in the form of cards, tea leaves, or anything else, you can tap into your chosen method of divination to assess predicted outcomes and deliver a more useful and accurate interpretation.

When we consider not only our own energy but also the energy of the moon, its documented effects on our planet (and on our lives), and tarot as an energetic conduit, then things get really interesting. Each moon phase has its own energy. The new moon, for instance, is a time of setting intentions and planting seeds for what we want to manifest in the cycle culminating with the full moon, which brings the lunar energy to its peak. In Pagan belief systems, the triple goddess is represented in the moon phases: new (maiden), full (mother), and waning (crone). These primal energies correspond with the phases of our lives. Just as we often plant seeds of intention during the new moon and harvest during the full moon, we release and clear energies during the waning moon. You can think of tarot as your energetic companion for every season of your life, just as the moon is always in the sky, in one form or another.

How to Make the Most of This Book

This book includes one chapter for each month, corresponding with each full moon, and an additional chapter for the blue moon, which occurs about once every two and a half years or so. Each chapter focuses on the energy of that month's full moon, and the spreads, rituals, and spells are devised around that energy. You can reference this book month by month, working with the spreads and performing the rituals with the corresponding moon phases as you move throughout the year, or you can use this book according to subject, depending on what you are working on and the guidance you are seeking at the moment. It isn't necessary to do all of the spreads and spells in the book or even to do them in the order they appear. You can reference them by subject and use them to provide guidance on any topic, any time of the year.

For example, if you have questions around a certain subject, such as love or career, you can turn to the index and look under the specific subject, such as *love* or *luck*. You can also search the table of contents for the spreads listed in each month. The beginning of each chapter mentions the overall energies for the month in the opening paragraph, and that energy informs all of the spreads and spells in that chapter. For instance, December's spreads are focused on taking a deep dive into your subconscious, connecting with your higher self, and tapping into your intuition to gain clarity and to guide you for the future. So if you are working on any of those things, regardless of the time of year, you can turn to those spreads to support you.

The spreads include suggested questions, and it is my hope that you will tailor those questions as you feel necessary and in ways that align with your particular situation and circumstances. You may feel compelled to ask a single question multiple times during a reading. For example, if you feel there may be more than one answer or factor at play, you can draw multiple cards for the same question. You may want to change the wording or add questions of your own to suit your needs. You can always draw a clarifying card if you'd like more information or want a deeper understanding of a particular card or query. The questions are intended as guidance, which you can use as written or adjust as you wish.

The same concept holds true when selecting spells and rituals. While they are listed by month according to the lunar energies they correspond with, it is by no means necessary to wait until March to do the ritual around planting new seeds. For example, December's rituals are for healing, cord cutting, and a house blessing, and you can, of course, use those any time they are useful to you. To find the spells and rituals that are relevant to what you are working on, turn to the index and search for your topic, such as *happiness*, for example. As with choosing a spread, you can also search the table of contents to choose a ritual by month, or select one according to the prevailing lunar energies for that month.

The spells and rituals in this book include suggestions for the ideal timing of the spell, or the day of the week and moon phase in which the energies would best support your work, but of course you won't always be able to time a spell for Monday during the new moon, for example. The suggestions are simply there for guidance, and if you find yourself in a matter of urgency that needs to be addressed during what would normally be considered an unfavorable time, chapter 7 includes an energetic shortcut that allows you to perform a spell at any time by neutralizing conflicting or contrasting influences (see "On the Timing of Spells and Rituals"). Remember that your intention has the most powerful influence over anything you do.

You might want to combine readings with spells. To do this, you can refer to the index for the particular subject you are focusing on, such as *positivity*. Because the spreads and spells in each month correspond with that month's lunar energy, spreads and spells within each chapter already hold corresponding energies and thematic influences, so you can easily combine readings and rituals that are grouped within the month. The opening paragraph to each chapter describes the prevailing energies for the month and will give you an idea of that month's theme.

Each chapter includes informative sidebars on topics related to tarot, rituals and spellwork, and other subjects that impact your practice. These include additional guidance to assist in your interpretation of a tarot reading by examining information such as repeating patterns and themes, and encourage you to reflect on the various aspects of energies associated with the spread to help you make the most of its interpretation and apply it most beneficially to your life.

The Stance of This Book

This book is written for those who wish to create change in their lives and for those who are interested in understanding themselves, their path, and the world around them, as well as their internal world, in greater depth. The spreads and rituals are devised to help you find clarity on a variety of subjects and to unveil layers of understanding through deeper connection, both to yourself and to the unseen energies around you. When it comes to foretelling future outcomes with the tarot, the cards can reveal how things will progress if circumstances continue on their current path. Typically, the outlook of a reading advances as far as three to six months ahead.

It is important to keep in mind that even the smallest of our actions and decisions can profoundly influence and alter the course of events; nothing is set in stone. We have the power to create change for ourselves. Through understanding the messages the cards reveal, we can choose to shift direction and take action to adjust outcomes in the way we desire. Meditation and rituals are powerful methods of creating change, setting intentions, and generating and directing energy toward a future manifestation.

This book is intended to be useful for all, regardless of background or belief system. It includes information on the law of attraction to support you with manifesting, and draws on Native American, Wiccan, and other Pagan ideologies and lore, and on concepts like feng shui. It is written from the belief that we are all one, that there is truth to be found everywhere—in every culture and belief system—and that we all share more similarities than differences. If something does not resonate with you, feel free to tailor it according to your preferences or simply take what is useful and disregard what isn't.

Interpreting the Tarot

Symbols are the language of the universe. Whether in the form of numbers, colors, or pictorial representations, they are tools of communication that the tarot makes great use of. Understanding the meaning behind the symbols can aid our interpretation and allow for greater depth of awareness and increased clarity.

Symbolic Correspondences

Tarot, being based on symbolism, draws from the wells of archetypal, numerological, and planetary representations, among so many others. Every part of the tarot is significant when it comes to the interpretation, and sometimes certain symbols, references, or correspondences will stand out more than others. You may have a deck for a while, then suddenly notice an aspect of a card you never realized was there. What is meant for us reaches us, provided we are open to receiving it. When something stands out to you, by all means, meditate on it or look it up; it may have wisdom of significance to impart to you. Following are some of the key symbologies to consider when interpreting a reading.

The Suits of the Tarot

Following is a guide denoting the element each suit is aligned with and its corresponding direction, the archangel associated with it, and what it generally represents. While this lists the traditional suits, as you explore different decks, you will find variations in the naming of the suits; some of those variations are listed under suit correspondences.

Pentacles

Element: Earth

Direction: North

Archangel: Uriel

Represents: The material realm, money, finances, wealth, home, property, business, health, physicality

Suit correspondences: Diamonds, disks, coins

Swords

Element: Air

Direction: East

Archangel: Raphael

Represents: The intellect, thinking, communication, logic, the mind, analysis, ambition

Suit correspondences: Spades, spears, pikes

Wands

Element: Fire

Direction: South

Archangel: Michael

Represents: The will, passion, manifestation, growth, personal power, spirit, motivation, energy, work and career

Suit correspondences: Clubs, batons, rods, staves, scepters, torches

Cups

Element: Water

Direction: West

Archangel: Gabriel

Represents: Emotions, love, feeling, intuition, reflection, compassion, the heart, relationships

Suit correspondences: Hearts, chalices, vessels

Court Cards

Court cards can represent people, or they can relate to a situation, surrounding energies and influences, aspects of the self, and events. Depending on the question and the circumstances, you will usually have a sense of which this is. For example, three queens appearing in a spread where the question is spiritually focused can indicate the support of guides, ancestors, or divine allies. It can also be helpful to consider the suits that appear in the reading (see table 1). If you receive the Queen of Swords and the Queen of Cups, this could indicate either a balance or a conflict between the head and the heart, depending on the other cards in the reading, the question, and the querent. Ultimately, connecting with your intuition is the most powerful tool at your disposal when interpreting meaning.

It can also be helpful to take into account the overall personas each court card represents:

Pages: Young person, developing personality; can indicate messages, information, the beginnings of a situation, naïveté, idealism.

Knights: Young adult; can indicate significant movement, travel, action, communication.

Queens: Motherly figures, women who have reached maturity; can indicate support, nurturing, feminine leadership, and authority.

Kings: Fatherly figures, mature men; can indicate masculine support, leadership, and authority.

Table 1: Indications of Multiple Court Cards in a Reading

# in Spread	Kings	Queens	Knights	Pages
2	Two energies, masculine in nature, possibly in competition with one another	Two energies, feminine in nature, that could be opposing or offering support	Two energies that may imply movement or competition	Two energies that may be competing for attention or encouraging choice
3	Brothers, close male relatives or friends, strong bonds between men; honor, recognition, accolades, awards	Sisters, close female relatives or friends, strong bonds between women; female allies and support	Friendships and social gatherings of young men; messages, information, and events	Celebrations and joyful gatherings of young people; youth
4	Male community or an organized group of men; gathering or meeting of significance	Female community or an organized group of women; influence of women	Competition or a team; rapid change on its way	Children, siblings, young peers or classmates; new beginnings and ideas

Numerological Correspondences

Galileo famously posited that math is the language of the universe and is what gives it structure; the more we discover, the more we find this to be true. This structure gives form to what would otherwise be chaos and ensures we are not "wandering about in a dark labyrinth," (Machamer, 1998, 65) as he noted. Numbers are conceptual, albeit very real, and they support and give structure to matter, which is a form of energy. When we consider that everything is energy, we can begin to comprehend the interconnectedness of everything—of every plant, animal, being, planet, star, galaxy, and beyond.

While some believe that each number is associated with specific attributes, others feel that numbers do not inherently hold any particular meaning, only what you assign to them. Certain numbers may mean certain things to you, and it is always recommended that you trust your intuition and your highest guidance. However, there are certain widely held associations that correspond with each number, and those are explored in table 2. These numeric correspondences can be useful in interpreting the meanings and symbolism of the tarot.

Table 2: Numeric Correspondences

1	New beginnings, manifestation, individuality
2	Partnerships, collaboration, cooperation, unity, balance
3	Manifestation, development, expression, celebration, creation, creativity
4	Solidity, foundations, structure, archangels, angels, organization, stability
5	Change, protection, shifts, uncertainty, conflict
6	Abundance, harmony, generosity, home, family, community
7	Luck, growth, spirituality, psychic ability, wisdom, visualization, focus, intellect
8	Abundance, success, expansion, accomplishment
9	Completion, wisdom
10	Endings and subsequent beginnings, success, fulfillment

Symbolism in the Tarot and Beyond

Throughout the tarot, you will find symbols that are associated with certain meanings, often of an archetypal nature, such as butterflies to indicate transformation. A single symbol can have multiple meanings, and it can mean something different to you at various times in your life. Ultimately, you should use your intuition to guide you, as you may perceive different symbolic meanings that are meant just for you, symbols that you may have a personal connection with. Some of the most commonly occurring symbols you will find in the tarot and their corresponding meanings can be found in the following list.

Tarot Symbols and Their Meanings

Acorn: Success, planning, preparation, reserves, wealth

Apple: Knowledge, prosperity

Arch: Passageways, options, openings, new directions

Arrow: • Pointing up can mean spirituality, elevation, or ascension
- Pointing down can indicate groundedness
- Pointing to the left or right can indicate physical directionality; in a tarot reading, consider what cards are to the left or right, or what the arrow is pointing to

Bear: Strength

Bell: News, weddings and marriages (if more than one bell)

Bird: Messenger, message, freedom, higher awareness, elevated thought, higher wisdom, ascension, ideals, goals

Blindfold: Intuition, self-limiting beliefs, blindness, refusal to see a situation for what it is or to face something, hidden truth

Book: Study, knowledge, wisdom

Bridge: Cooperation, collaboration, connection, peace, reconciliation, moving from one phase of life into another, options, solutions

Butterfly: Transformation, metamorphosis, spiritual immortality

Castle: Home, stability, foundations, support, goals

Cat: Cunning, cleverness, intuition, perception, need for awareness, psychic ability

Children: Hope, promise, new beginnings, family, joy, innocence, renewal, new ideas

Circle: Completion, continuity, unity, protection, wholeness, the eternal

Clouds: Revelations, the divine, higher thought, divine assistance and messages, epiphanies, clouded judgment or confusion (depending on appearance and context)

Cross: Religion, integration, manifestation

Crown: Sovereignty, success, fame, wealth, status, leadership, victory, mastery

Cup: Water element, goddess, receiving, divine feminine, knowledge, love

Deer: Gentleness, caution, trusting your instincts, grace

Dog: Loyalty, faithfulness, domesticity, truth, fidelity

Dove: Peace, promises, hope, making amends, purity, ascension, love

Egg: New life, fertility, gestation, birth

Feather: Air element, angels, divine assistance, divine communication

Fire: Passion, will, transformation, power, ambition, energy

Fish: Abundance, idea, thought, creativity, emotion, intuition

Flag: Major changes, shifts, and transformation; freedom

Flowers: Red: beauty, romance, love; White: Purity, innocence, hope, new beginnings; Yellow: Joy, prosperity, happiness

Frog: Abundance, fertility, transformation, release, rebirth, renewal

Fruit: Fertility, abundance

Grapes: Abundance, blessings, fertility, prosperity, pleasure

Horse: Forward motion, vitality, strength, vigor, action

Key: Esoteric knowledge, secret wisdom, accessing what is hidden, unlocking potential

Lantern or torch: Leadership, guidance, wisdom, knowledge, illumination, truth, understanding, hope, intelligence, clarity

Lemniscate: Eternal life, infinity, continuity

Lightning: Swift change, sudden movement, divine intervention

Lily: Health, fertility, growth, purity, innocence

Lion: Strength, leadership, authority, courage, protection

Lobster: Protection, regeneration

Moon: Intuition, psychic ability, reflection, the hidden, secrets, change, development, gestation, femininity, time, cycles, the subconscious

Mountain: Pinnacle, achievement, triumph, summit, vision, success, reaching new heights, challenge

Olive branch: Peace, promise, unity, reconciliation

Path: Journey, direction, beginnings, next steps, choices

Pentacle: Earth element, protection, wealth, material realm

Pillar: Balance, diplomacy, perspective, principles

Pomegranate: Divine feminine, abundance, beauty, passion, fertility, death, eternal life

Pumpkin: Prosperity, abundance, harvest

Rabbit: Quickness, groundedness, fertility, abundance, family

Rainbow: Hope, joy, unity, new beginnings, promise, celebration, renewal

Ram: Leadership, authority, determination, action, resolve, initiative

Salamander or lizard: Fire element, rebirth, renewal, vision, enlightenment

Scales: Balance, justice

Scepter: Leadership, wisdom, authority, direction, power

Shell: Water element, beauty, femininity, divine feminine, prosperity, abundance, love, mystery

Ship or boat: Travel, smooth sailing ahead, departure, leaving a situation, moving

Snake: Movement, transformation, renewal, secret knowledge, flexibility, subtlety, wisdom, self-knowledge

Spiral: Life force, universal energies, regeneration, movement, creation, growth, connection to Source, motion, progress, development

Square: Structure, foundations, solidity, stability, earth, manifestation

Star: Hope, new beginnings, promise

Sun: Joy, optimism, bright future, happiness, masculinity

Sunflower: Happiness, joy, abundance

Swan: Grace, beauty

Sword or knife: Air element, intellect, knowledge, clarity, intelligence, logic, communication

Tree: Growth, protection, wisdom, connection to earth/Gaia, knowledge, fortitude

Triangle: Trinity; pointing upward indicates fire or air and the divine masculine; pointing downward indicates earth or water and the divine feminine

Trumpet: Announcements, news, messages, rebirth, awakening, major change, triumph, victory, celebrations

Villages: Group efforts, common goals, team efforts, community, harmony, security, protection

Wand: Willpower, manifestation, assertion

Water: Flow, ease, intuition, psyche, secret knowledge, depth, emotions, mystery, subconscious

Preparation for Spells and Rituals

Tools of divination, such as tarot, and tools of directing the will, such as wands and athames, are used in ritual space alongside allies and methodologies that support your manifestations, such as herbs, crystals, meditation, and the writing of intentions. Throughout this book, you will find tips on manifestation and on working with the tarot. Some spells require fewer tools than others, but if you find yourself ready for a ritual and short on supplies, you are encouraged to make substitutions where possible. Ultimately, your will alone is sufficient to create any change you desire; the tools are there to support you with their energies. While they can lend power to rituals, they are not strictly necessary. Just be sure to look up any substitutions before using them in your rituals, as every crystal, herb, and physical object has its own unique energy; you don't want to bring in any elements that will counteract your intentions.

The appendices include a protection meditation and an all-purpose, customizable ritual ("Appendix B: Amplifying Your Intentions: A Full Moon Ritual") that includes language you can use for casting a circle of protection, calling the quarters, working with the elements, and so on. When it comes to protecting yourself, your vibration ultimately determines what you allow to reach you. When you raise your vibration, you are not visible or accessible to energies of a lower vibration, so where you are vibrating at any given moment determines what you are allowing in. That being said, circles of protection are always a good idea and are recommended every time you do ritual work, as they create a sacred space that forms a boundary around you and protects you, your energy, your ritual space, and all the energies within it. Think of it as an energetic container.

Days of the Week and Corresponding Energies

Each day of the week is associated with different planetary influences and carries its own particular energy. When you have an understanding of the energies that are supporting your manifestations, you can easily tailor existing rituals and devise your own.

Sunday

Associated with the sun, which has a masculine energy, this day supports expansion, wealth, business and career-related endeavors, educational advancement, promotions, investments, achievements, empowerment, wellness, goal setting, joyful activities, and celebrations of all kinds.

Monday

This day is associated with the moon, which has a feminine energy and supports inward-looking activities such as psychic expansion, past-life regressions, connecting to and strengthening intuition, and tuning in to the divine. Also supported are fertility, beauty, emotions, healing, medicine, the home, family, gardening, psychic work, wisdom, and divination.

Tuesday

The planet Mars, which rules Tuesday, is named after the Roman god of war. Accordingly, this is a great day to work on anything related to passion, physicality, courage, confidence, strength, protection, initiations, and new beginnings. Tuesday's energy also supports test-taking, job-seeking, and surgical procedures.

Wednesday

Mercury rules Wednesday; if you think of the word *mercurial,* you get the idea. This is the day for anything related to communication, work and career, research, making travel plans, the arts, and creating change. Wednesday, with its midweek positioning, is ideal for creating shifts, tying up loose ends, and working with transitions and transitional energies.

Thursday

Named after Thor, this day is associated with Jupiter and supports anything related to health, strength, socializing, awards, self-improvement, travel, abundance, luck, prosperity, and getting things resolved. Because Thursday supports achievement, development, and vitality, this is an auspicious time to take tests and to work with doctors, therapists, healers, and legal counsel.

Friday

The planet Venus rules Friday, and Friday derives its name from the goddess Freya, who is associated with love and fertility. This day supports anything related to love, romance, fertility, dating, unity, collaborations, social events and socializing, music, relaxation, fun, creativity, reconciliation, decorating, and revitalizing your physical space.

Saturday

This day belongs to Saturn, the Roman god associated with agriculture, generation, wealth, and renewal, who was later identified with the Greek god of time, Chronos. Saturday supports banishments, endings, the cutting of ties, clearing, cleansing, releasing, transformation, and protection.

The Influences and Qualities of the Moon Phases

The moon is ever-changing, and its position relative to earth and the sun determines the amount of light it reflects. Because sunlight delivers energy to our planet, as the phases of the moon shift, so do the moon's vibrational qualities and the ways it affects us. Below are the energetic correspondences for each phase of the moon, which you can use as a guide for timing your rituals and spellwork.

Dark

Also known as the balsamic moon, this is the time before the new moon when no light is visible. It is a time to look within, reflect, meditate, and assess where you have been, where you are, and where you want to be. The dark moon is a potent time for journeywork, past-life regression, protection, and enhancing psychic abilities and intuition.

New

The moon moves from darkness into the first sliver of light as the new cycle is becoming. This is a time to plant seeds of manifestation and begin new projects. During this time, perform rituals aligned with new beginnings and write out your intentions in a journal or in a sacred space.

Waxing

The moon is growing, and the amount of light it reflects increases day by day until it reaches the full moon phase. The waxing moon's energy supports expansion of any kind. During this time, focus on new endeavors, boosting your health, income, promotions, raises, new jobs, growing your family, love, romance, and anything else you want to increase.

First Quarter

As the energies of the moon begin to grow, from the time the moon is new to the waxing half-moon phase, we begin expanding in awareness, clarity, overall sensitivity, and in our clairgifts and empathic abilities. During this time, pay special attention to symbols and dreams that feel significant, as they may have messages for you, whether from your subconscious or from your allies. This is the ideal time to tune in to the messages and symbols you are receiving to gain awareness and insight.

Second Quarter

From the time of the first quarter, or waxing half moon, until the full moon, our senses are moving up the dial toward total amplification at the peak of the phase. The closer we get to the full moon, the more our senses and abilities are turned up, like turning up the volume on a radio. The messages of dreams and intuition can be powerful during this time, making it a great period to tap into divination, whether through tools, processes, rituals, or by looking within.

Full

Lunar energy reaches its peak and reflects the sun's light across the entire visible surface in the full moon phase. Likewise, this is when projects and manifestations increase to a point of fullness. Seeds planted during the new moon and waxing moon have grown and are ready to be born. Full moon energy is powerful and amplifies your intentions and the energy generated from rituals performed during this time. The full moon enhances psychic awareness and is a great time for celebrations.

Waning

After the expansion and peak energy of the full moon passes, the amount of light reflected continues to wane, or decrease, as it reaches toward the dark moon. This is a time of clearing, releasing, and letting go. The waning energy is ideal for cutting cords and working on things such as weight loss, ending relationships, and removing unwanted energies and obstacles.

Third Quarter

From just after the full moon until the time of the waning half moon, as the light decreases, greater emphasis is placed on what is hidden. While this is an ideal time for clearing and releasing unwanted energies and situations, it is also a time that rewards meditation and inner reflection. During this period, tune in to your heart and consider what your spirit is calling you to.

Fourth Quarter

From the waning half moon to the time before the new moon, the lunar light decreases until nothing is visible. During this period, people tend to be affected differently, either tuning in more sharply to their psychic and divinatory abilities, or experiencing a decreased connection to them. Regardless of which end of the spectrum you lean toward, during this time, inner reflection, deep contemplation, and exploration of the psyche is supported, which may bring increased insight, growth, and clarity, either now or in the future.

Unique Moons

Blue Moon

Besides denoting something unique or rare, a blue moon is the third full moon in a season that has four or, according to a more recent definition, the second full moon in a month. Seasonal blue moons happen about once every two and a half years. Chapter 13 is dedicated to the blue moon and includes rituals that embrace the amplified energy of this bonus moon.

Supermoon

A supermoon occurs about once every fourteen months or so, when the full moon is at its closest point to earth. Its proximity makes it look larger than usual, hence its name. Supermoons can appear up to 14 percent brighter, and their impact on the tides increases by up to 18 percent. With so much additional energy impacting us, these moons are powerful times for performing meditations and rituals.

Blood Moon

The moon's red appearance during this time is the result of reflected light from the earth's surface following a total lunar eclipse. An eclipse can be thought of as an energetic reset, and the time following it can be valuable for tuning in and gaining greater insight and awareness, especially when you are working on shifting your energy, shifting the energies of a situation, or seeking illumination regarding making changes or taking a different path.

Black Moon

If the blue moon has a counterpart, it's the black moon. A black moon can be the third new moon in a season that has four new moons or the second new moon in a month. (This term is also used to refer to a month without a full moon and to a month without a new moon.) Much as the blue moon enhances the energy of the full moon, black moon energy supports a twice-deeper dive into the realms of the subconscious and empowers new intentions with enhanced fertility.

Mini Moon

The mini moon, sometimes also called a micro moon, is the counterpart to the supermoon and occurs when the full moon is at its farthest point from Earth. This wee moon appears about 8 percent smaller and its luminosity is decreased by around 15 percent. It is associated with a lessening of the typical full moon energy and a corresponding decreased impact to psychic awareness and manifestational developments. If you find yourself needing more of an impact during a mini moon, you can add energy to your work with the full moon amplification ritual in appendix B.

Color Correspondences

Each color has certain energetic correspondences that can support your intentions. The elements are also associated with certain colors, and in the spells and rituals throughout this book, specific colors are used to align with particular outcomes. When you want to tailor a spell to your liking or create your own ritual, knowledge of the color correspondences is helpful, as you can bring in more of a certain color to energetically support your work. The meaning of colors can vary among cultures, traditions, and belief systems, but below are some universal interpretations.

Table 3: Color Correspondences

Black	power, banishment, releasing, protection, subconscious, wisdom
White	purity, purification, divinity, protection, integrity, spirituality, transformation, healing, beginnings, peace, amplification, all-purpose
Brown	earth, groundedness, stability, fortitude, protection of home and property, animals
Red	passion, fire, courage, vitality, strength, ambition, willpower, vigor, sexuality, charisma
Pink	self-love, healing, love, devotion, friendship, connection, romance, affection, unconditional love, partnerships, femininity
Orange	energy, confidence, achievement, change, warmth, power, creativity, self-control, order, courage
Yellow	optimism, expansion, joy, creativity, friendship, happiness, well-being, logic, learning, memory
Green	earth, growth, money, wealth, abundance, healing, fertility, health, work, career
Light Blue	clarity, calm, ease, compassion, confidence, truth, knowledge, communication, harmony
Dark Blue	inspiration, sovereignty, perception, leadership, astral projection, loyalty
Purple	intuition, power, psychic abilities, wisdom, spirituality, independence, divination
Lavender	serenity, calm, psychic abilities, divination, communication with spirit

Chapter 1
January: The Wolf Moon

Also referred to as the Ice Moon, the Snow Moon, the Old Moon, or the Moon after Yule, January's Wolf Moon is named after the howling wolves that sound their cry during this wintry time of the year.

The Wolf Moon tarot spreads included in this chapter are designed to help you discover your untapped potential, what lies frozen beneath the surface, and what is dormant and awaiting a resurgence. You will also dive deep to find what is calling you, gain clarity on what may be stuck or trapped within you, and explore the finer nuances of your connections with others through a relationship renewal spread.

The spells and rituals in this chapter help you shift the energies around you, allowing you to empower yourself, make your voice heard, and to free whatever may be stuck in your life.

The Deep Dive: Upon Further Examination

The suggested questions provided with the spreads throughout this book are intended as starting points—conversation starters, one might say, in the discussion between you and the universal forces that are providing the answers you seek. These questions may spark ideas for questions of your own, and you may wish to tailor the questions to address your specific situation.

Sometimes, you will receive a card that seems to raise more questions than it answers. When this happens, it is advisable to go off trail from the suggested questions or from what you had in mind to ask and formulate new inquiries that address the particular energies of that card. You can always draw a clarifying card and return to where you were in the questioning process. When what is revealed leads to more questions, it can take you down an invaluable path of discovery, if you simply follow it. That is, after all, why we use tarot: to delve deeper into the mystery, to look beyond, to explore, to expand and enhance our understanding, and to seek guidance, wisdom, and clarity.

Spreads

Tapping into Your Potential

Use this spread (see illustration 1-1) to discover your untapped potential and uncover any dormant talents or gifts. This spread is also useful for helping to shine a light on areas of your life that would benefit from your attention. For example, if you are trying to choose a career path and you are good at several things, use this spread to reveal the direction that would be most beneficial for you to follow.

Suggested questions:

1. What is an area of untapped potential in my life?
2. What are my greatest gifts?
3. Where would it be most beneficial for me to focus now?
4. What steps can I take to start developing my potential?
5. How can I best put my potential to use?
6. In what areas of my life will it benefit me?
7. How can I use it to benefit others?

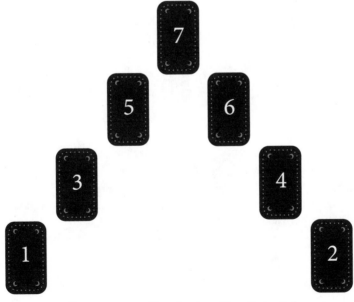

Illustration 1-1: Tapping into Your Potential

Shuffling and Drawing Tarot Cards

Shuffling a tarot deck as you would shuffle a regular pack of cards is considered disrespectful by many tarot readers, as a tarot deck is a sacred tool meant for connection with the divine and is deserving of being handled with respect. A preferred way to shuffle a tarot deck is overhand, using both hands to mix up the cards, moving them over and under each other at random. Some readers like to spread out the cards and then choose them as they are guided.

Before drawing a card, focus on the question by keeping it in your mind as you shuffle, or you can ask your question aloud. You may choose to pull a card from the top, or you can shuffle until one or more cards fall out. Some readers prefer the latter method, as more than one card can be necessary to provide a more complete response to a question, and letting the universe deliver as many cards as are needed is ideal, as it can give you the full scope of an answer and a more complete picture of a situation.

If you are drawing cards from the top of the deck, many see the "jumpers," or cards that jump out of the deck during shuffling, as significant to the reading. These cards may give you the answer you're looking for but haven't yet asked about, they may offer additional or supporting information, or they can signify an aspect you may not have considered—the answer to a question you may not have asked. The card on the bottom of the deck, after you have finished shuffling and drawing your cards, is a foundational or baseline card that informs the reading with its influence.

What Lies Beneath

This spread (see illustration 1-2) reveals energies, aspects, and situations that may be hidden. Use it to uncover the underlying elements of a situation, to discover the driving forces behind something, and to better understand any unseen factors. You can also tailor the questions to find out what is frozen or stuck in certain areas of your life and why something isn't moving forward.

Suggested questions:

1. Please reveal the nature of a situation that is hidden from me (or frozen, or stuck).
2. What are its prevalent aspects?
3. Who or what is behind it?
4. Why has it been hidden from me?
5. What can I learn from this situation?
6. How can this situation benefit me?
7. How is this situation currently developing?
8. What actions are best for me to take at this time?
9. How can I resolve the situation?
10. What else do I need to know?

Illustration 1-2: What Lies Beneath

Awakening Dormant Energies

Discover how to awaken, energize, and activate dormant energies with this spread (see illustration 1-3), and how to give yourself the best chances for success—whether the energies in question have to do with career, business, finance, relationships, home, family, or spiritual aspects.

Suggested questions:

1. Please reveal the dormant energies that are ready to be awakened in my life.
2. How can I breathe life into them?
3. In what area of my life are these energies best applied?
4. What is the best way for me to begin moving forward with this?
5. What actions are most beneficial for me to take at this time?
6. A message from my higher self.

Illustration 1-3: Awakening Dormant Energies

What Is Calling You

If you have been busy or feeling overwhelmed, if you feel you could use some clarity, or if you are ready to begin a new project, this spread (see illustration 1-4) can help shine a light on where it would be most beneficial for you to focus. Use it to uncover what in your life is calling for your attention right now, and where you can best focus your efforts.

Suggested questions:

1. What is calling for my attention?
2. What is an area of opportunity for me?
3. Where would it benefit me to focus now?
4. What will focusing on this bring me?
5. How can I best apply my energies?
6. What can I do to bring this to fruition?
7. What can I do to make this a success?
8. What else do I need to know about this?
9. A message from my higher self.

Illustration 1-4: What Is Calling You

Freeing What Is Trapped

Whether you wish to release relationships, cut ties, or unbind yourself from a situation, this spread (see illustration 1-5) helps to shine a light on the most beneficial ways to clear, release, and transmute (or heal) what is not serving you. It can also be helpful for gaining clarity on what needs to be released and can guide you through what to do to free stuck or trapped energies, even if you are not entirely certain what they are or where they came from.

Suggested questions:

1. What am I holding on to that isn't working for me?
2. What needs to be cleared out of my life now?
3. How can I release what isn't working?
4. How can I completely clear out the energies that need to leave my life now?
5. How can I best move forward after clearing and releasing the energies?
6. What needs healing in light of this release?
7. What can I learn from this situation?
8. A message from my guides.

Illustration 1-5: Freeing What Is Trapped

The Power of Intention

Never underestimate the power of intention. Science tells us that everything is made of energy—even our thoughts. Teachers such as Esther Hicks, who shares the Abraham-Hicks teachings, explain that we create our own realities through our thoughts, which first establish a vibrational reality that then manifests into tangible, physical reality. We are constantly shaping our lives through our beliefs, the ways in which we focus our minds, and where and how we direct our thoughts. So you quite literally are what you think.

The tradition of saying a prayer or mantra or setting an intention while lighting a candle is an ancient practice that spans centuries, cultures, and belief systems. Simply lighting a candle is one way of focusing the mind toward a certain intention. For example, asking for healing or sending healing to a loved one while focusing on the flame concentrates the energy of the thought or intention, thereby focusing the power of the energy.

Whatever you focus on or think about fills your vibration. And, because of the law of attraction—which says that like attracts like—similar energies are drawn to you. This principle is responsible for bringing to you whatever you are an energetic match for, which is whatever you hold in your vibration, which stems from your thoughts and beliefs. And a belief, Abraham-Hicks tells us, is simply a thought that you continue to think.

Relationship Renewal

Relationships can ebb and flow, progress and stagnate, and the dynamic of energy between two people is often complex. Use this spread (see illustration 1-6) to understand the inner workings of a relationship and its nuances, how you can establish clarity of communication and address any issues, and explore how you can renew and refresh the energies of any relationship, platonic or romantic.

First, pull a card representing you and place it in what will be the center of the spread. Then, pull a card representing the person you are querying about and focus on them a moment before beginning. Place their card next to yours in the center.

Suggested questions:

1. A card representing our relationship.
2. A card representing our communication.
3. A card representing how this person feels about me.
4. A card representing how I feel about this person.
5. What should I know about this person?
6. What should I know about our relationship?
7. A card representing what is working.
8. A card representing what is not working.
9. How can I best address our issues?
10. How can we reenergize our bonds?
11. Where is clarity needed?
12. What is the best action I can take at this time?

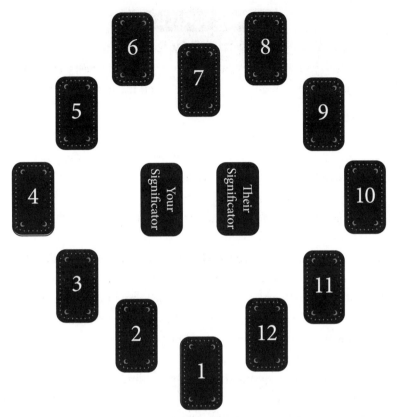

Illustration 1-6: Relationship Renewal

Spells & Rituals
I Step into My Power

Use this spell anytime you want to expand in your power. It's best performed on a Sunday, ideally during a full moon, but also effective when the moon is new or waxing.

What You Need:
One white candle
Olive oil
A dash of cayenne (for strength and empowerment)
A pinch of motherwort (for courage)
A pinch of artemisia (mugwort; for confidence and courage)

Before beginning, create a sacred space (see appendix B) and ground by using your intention to send any and all stuck and trapped energies and energies that are not serving you down into the earth to be transmuted (see appendix A for a full grounding meditation). Intend that these energies are cleared and released from your field. Visualize and feel them leaving you as they move down through the foundations (if you are indoors) and into the earth to be neutralized.

Close your eyes and picture golden-white light filling your energetic field and surrounding you in a high-vibrational sphere of protection. With your eyes still closed, "see" into the light that surrounds you and scan your field for anything that is not serving you. You may see this as strands, cords, or flecks that are dark in color. Envision them being encompassed by blindingly bright, pure golden-white light, dissolving and transmuting into energy of the highest possible vibration; some may simply leave your field entirely. You can always call on your allies to support you during this process.

As you are doing this, you may notice sensations in your body; these may be indications of where energy has been lodged that is not serving you. Send this energy down into the earth simply by intending it, and visualize that area of your body filling with light and healing. You may feel a cooling sensation as the energy leaves you and warmth as the light fills and heals the area. Continue this process until the sphere around you is clear and you feel you have addressed all areas needing attention in your physical body.

Set the intention that this protective sphere remains around you and that only high-vibrational energies may enter and only high-vibrational energies may remain within this sphere. It is a good idea to surround yourself with the sphere of protection on a regular basis and always before beginning any ritual or meditation. Many find it helpful to begin each day with this practice, surrounding themselves with protective light and clearing the energetic field whenever needed (see appendix A).

If you have not already, call on any allies you may be working with and set the intention that only high-vibrational energies are allowed around you, or simply call in support that is in alignment with your highest good. Coat the candle with olive oil and roll it in the cayenne, motherwort, and artemisia, ensuring that it is fully coated.

Light the candle and state confidently, either aloud or silently:

I step into my power. I connect with my higher self and call upon my highest truth. I am filled with my highest power, with the fullness of my Source energy as I remember who I am. I call my highest wisdom to me now. I call my higher knowledge to me now. I allow the truth of who I am to fill my mind, to fill my being, to fill my understanding as every cell of my body resonates with my truth. I am becoming the most powerful version of myself. I am becoming fully empowered and expanding in my truth. I am powerful.

With your eyes closed, let the flame of the candle fill your field of vision. With your intention, expand the light of the flame until it fills and surrounds your entire energetic field. Feel its power expanding within you. Think of the flame as a powerful piece of the sun, which warms the entire planet with its light. Envision the light of the sun filling you and surrounding you and expanding within you.

Then envision yourself living your most fully empowered life. Really see yourself as the best possible version of you, visualizing everything from how you carry yourself to how you dress, where you live, what vehicle you drive, how you spend your time, and who your friends are.

It is to your benefit to take your time with this ritual and visualize it as vividly as possible. You can repeat it as often as you feel guided. The beauty of repeating it is that, with each repetition, you are strengthening the visualization and further empowering yourself.

When you are done meditating and visualizing, let the candle burn all the way down. Tip: Chimes candles are readily available online and in magical provisions shops and typically burn in one to several hours, so are ideal to use for spells.

My Voice Is Heard

Use this spell to amplify your voice and ensure you speak your truth from a place of alignment. Best performed on a Tuesday or Wednesday during a waxing moon.

What You Need:
Cayenne (for strength and empowerment)
Turmeric (for strength and vitality)
Thyme (for courage and communication)
A spoonful of honey (to sweeten the speech)
Hot water (drinkable temperature)
A teacup

Heat the water and add the ingredients above to the water—how much you add is up to you—and stir to create a mixture that you will drink. Take a moment to ground as the ingredients steep (see appendix A for a full grounding meditation), then get clear on your intention to make your voice heard.

Sip the tea and say (aloud or to yourself, but aloud is better for this spell):

When I speak, people listen. My voice is heard by whomever I wish to hear it. I am heard and I am understood in the ways I intend to be heard and understood. I am taken seriously. I am respected and I treat others with respect. I carry myself with integrity. I speak with intention, I speak with clarity, and I choose my words carefully. My words align with my intentions, and my intentions are always clear. I always speak from a place of truth and authenticity. My words are meaningful. My voice is strong and powerful. What I say matters. I make a difference.

Then, finish the tea, and as you sip, sit with the truth of the words you have just spoken and feel into this truth until you know that it is done. Remember that the past is the past; just because something has been a certain way before does not mean it has to be true anymore. Give yourself permission to let go of anything from the past you may be holding on to, including any guilt or resentment, and forgive yourself and others. Every now moment is a chance for a fresh start and a chance to welcome the new. Every heartbeat is a new beginning.

I Open the Cage of My Heart: Freeing What Is Trapped

Use this ritual to release the energies that do not serve you, and surround yourself with protection. Best performed on a Saturday during a waning moon or the dark moon.

What You Need:
A tarot card representing you (your significator)
The Sun tarot card
One white candle
A piece of paper (or more, if needed)
A pen
A cauldron or other vessel in which to safely burn the paper

If you are performing this indoors, it is best to do so in a room with no artificial lights on. Place the card representing you in front of the unlit candle, and keep the Sun card available, as you will place it atop your significator card later. Write all of your burdens on the paper, inscribing everything that comes into your mind that is bothering you and that you wish to clear, release, and transmute from your heart, mind, and vibration.

After you have finished writing, light the candle and say:

I open the cage of my heart and release what does not serve my highest good. I clear, release, and transmute all energies that do not serve my highest good from my heart, from my mind, and from my energy field. I clear, release, and transmute all energies within me that are stuck or trapped that do not serve me. I clear and release them from my vibration and send them into the earth to be transmuted. I clear, release, and transmute them from every layer and level of my being and existence, across all times, dimensions, space, and realities. I clear, release, and transmute all cords, ties, attachments, anchors, hooks, streamers, thoughtforms, and all energies that do not serve my highest good. I clear and release all energies that do not serve my highest good and send them into the earth to be transmuted. This process continues until all energies that do not serve my highest good are cleared, released, and transmuted.

Sit with this feeling a while until you are ready to proceed; you may feel energies physically leaving your body or a gradually increasing sense of lightness. Or you may simply sense when it is time to continue. When you are ready, light the paper and place it in the cauldron or vessel to safely burn.

Then say: *I am a clear vessel. I am free. My heart is free and clear. I am connected to my highest good. I am aligned with my inner being.* Place the Sun card over your significator. Close your eyes and visualize the light of the flame filling your field and surrounding you—cleansing, purifying, and healing you. Imagine its warmth encompassing you like the heat of the sun. Imagine this as a golden sphere that originates within your heart and expands outward as it clears harmful energies and surrounds you in a powerful layer of protection. This protection cannot be breached and immediately blocks and stops all harmful energies and energies that are not in alignment with your highest good. The sphere should expand past your fingertips when you have your arms outstretched. Intend that all energies the sphere blocks and stops are transmuted. This ensures that they are not still lingering around you. Reinforce this sphere daily and as often as you feel you need to.

Say:

My heart is not a cage but is filled with my high-vibrational energy. I open my heart and invite the pure Source energy of my higher self to fill the entirety of my being. Light of the highest vibration fills me and expands within me and all around me, encompassing me completely in a powerful sphere of protection that can never be breached. I am filled with high-vibrational light. I am filled with joy. I am filled with peace. I am filled with clarity. I am safe and protected at all times.

Let the candle safely burn all the way down until it extinguishes on its own. You may wish to sit and meditate with it until it burns completely, or simply go on with your day, strong in your knowing that this work is done.

Chapter 2
FEBRUARY: THE SNOW MOON

The Native North American tribes who gave the full moons the sobriquets we know today sometimes called February's full moon the Ice Moon, or the Hunger Moon, because of the scarcity of food during this wintry time. It is also referred to as the Storm Moon, but more commonly it is known as the Snow Moon.

The Snow Moon tarot spreads included in this chapter explore what is causing lack, how to bring in abundance, making room for expansion in your life, where excess could be trimmed, and opportunities for nourishment on an energetic level.

The spells and rituals in this chapter include creating a talisman to draw in abundance, a magical infusion to expand your capacity for wealth, cutting ties with what does not serve you, and healing a compromised aura.

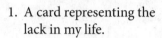

Spreads

Uncover Sources of Lack

Whether you are aware of certain areas of your life that just never seem to reach fulfillment or their full potential—whether it is related to money, career, or relationships—or if you feel that something is missing but find it difficult to pinpoint exactly what that is, use this spread (see illustration 2-1) to uncover any sources of lack, to find what is missing in your life, and to reveal where you might be blocking things from coming to you.

Suggested questions:

1. A card representing the lack in my life.
2. What is causing this?
3. How can I correct it?
4. A card representing what is missing for me.
5. Why is it missing?
6. How can I let in what is missing?
7. Where am I creating blockages?
8. Where could my mindset use adjusting?
9. How can I receive what I am asking for?
10. A message from my higher self.

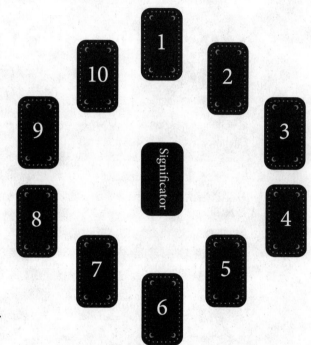

Illustration 2-1: Uncover Sources of Lack

Reflecting on Your Reading

As you continue to work with the tarot over time and gain familiarity with the nuances and various meanings of the cards, you will develop an instinct—if you have not already—that will help you to readily understand how the cards apply to your life, the messages they are bringing you, and what wisdom they are reflecting in your life. You may notice certain cards coming up for you often; these can signify certain ongoing aspects or they can represent particular people or situations in your life. Sometimes, a card will keep coming up for you until its meaning is fully understood.

One thing to look for is repeating patterns and themes. Did you pull mostly swords or multiple sevens, for example? Numbers have certain meanings associated with them (see the introduction for a glimpse into numerological interpretations). Was more than one person depicted on the cards in your reading holding a wand or a sword? This could signify new opportunities or clarity.

Looking for subtleties, such as whether any of the people or animals in the cards are facing each other or turned in opposite directions, can also provide deeper insight. Any symbolism on the cards, like archetypal symbols, butterflies, or animals, can also be revealing; see the introduction for a chart of symbols and their meanings.

Calling in Abundance

Abundance can apply to many areas of life—money, spiritual harmony, friendships, career, love, family relationships, fun, creativity, material possessions, nourishment of all kinds, and so much more. We are all worthy of abundance, but sometimes our personal beliefs get in the way of letting it in or we can block it unintentionally. Whether this is the case, or if you simply want to bring in more abundance, this spread (see illustration 2-2) can help you gain clarity and insight to help you live the life you deserve and desire.

Suggested questions:

1. Gratitude card: abundance already in my life that I can focus on to draw more to me.

2. Where am I blocking my abundance?

3. How can I draw in more abundance overall?

4. Where can I shift my focus to draw more abundance to me?

5. Low-hanging fruit: What is ripe and ready for the picking?

6. What seeds can I nurture that will bear fruit for me down the road?

7. Where should I focus my attention for longer-term abundance?

8. A hidden opportunity for abundance.

9. How can I establish and/ or strengthen an abundance mindset?

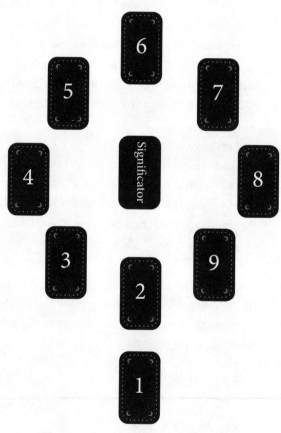

Illustration 2-2: Calling in Abundance

Making Room for Expansion

Life is an exercise in expansion—we are always learning, growing, receiving, and discovering new information, wisdom, and understanding, and constantly pinpointing new goals and desires, whether or not we consciously realize it. This spread (see illustration 2-3) is helpful if you are looking for clarity on current areas of expansion in your life, if you wish to identify new paths of opportunity, if you want to know where more expansion is ready to take place, and how you can receive more of what you are calling to you.

Suggested questions:

1. Where am I currently expanding?
2. Where am I doing especially well?
3. Where do I need to grow?
4. Where am I limiting myself?
5. What is ready for expansion in my life?
6. How can I increase my capacity to receive?
7. How can I allow in more of what I seek?
8. What are some areas of opportunity for me?

Illustration 2-3: Making Room for Expansion

Trimming the Fat

At times, we can feel energetically sluggish, have a general sense of malaise, or feel weighed down. Often, when this happens, we aren't sure of the cause—it's just a feeling that persists. Use this spread (see illustration 2-4) to gain clarity on anything that needs to be excised from your life, the best way to go about clearing it, and what you should focus on fortifying once this is done.

Suggested questions:

1. Where is there excess in my life?
2. What needs clearing from my life physically?
3. What needs clearing spiritually?
4. What needs clearing mentally?
5. What is the best way for me to clear this energy or situation?
6. Where would it benefit me to cut back?
7. What are some areas where it would benefit me to make adjustments?
8. What do I need to strengthen?

Illustration 2-4: Trimming the Fat

The Art and Science of Meditation

Because we are both physical and nonphysical beings, maintaining the balance of body, mind, and spirit is important to our overall health. Practices like meditation nourish the spirit like food nourishes the body, and are effective in replenishing stamina when your energy feels low. These are among the reasons many practitioners meditate on a daily basis, especially at the beginning of the day. If you need a quick recharge or uplift, sitting for even a short period of time and simply quieting the mind, focusing on your breath, can give you the boost you need.

Science is catching on to the health benefits of meditation, as researchers are finding that the practice is effective in treating both physical and mental conditions—everything from psoriasis to PTSD. Researchers analyzed the brain scans of patients who started practicing meditation and noted that they experience enduring results that positively affect their brains even when they are not meditating. Those patients demonstrated heightened emotional stability and a decreased response to stress, thus confirming what ancient wisdom has held for centuries.

Opportunities for Nourishment

If you feel that there is a drain on your energy or that certain areas of your life would benefit from being reenergized, use this spread (see illustration 2-5) to pinpoint what is causing your energy to be depleted, to understand any present sources of spiritual and energetic nourishment, and how you can reenergize yourself. It is also useful for helping you to gain clarity on any unseen opportunities and changes you could make that would be beneficial to you.

Suggested questions:

1. What is nourishing me spiritually?
2. What is nourishing my energy?
3. What is causing my energy to be depleted?
4. Where do I need to nourish myself more?
5. How can I reenergize myself?
6. Where do I need to fortify myself?
7. What changes can I make to strengthen myself?
8. What source of nourishment is available to me that I'm not seeing?
9. What are some opportunities that would assist me that I'm not seeing?
10. A message from my guides.

Illustration 2-5: Opportunities for Nourishment

Cleansing and Charging Your Crystals

There are a variety of ways to cleanse and charge your crystals. Just as you keep your belongings clean, it is important to periodically cleanse crystals of energetic buildup, as even high-vibrational crystals, such as selenite, can absorb negative energy. As you would plug in your phone to recharge its battery, it is important to charge, or reenergize, your crystals.

Cleansing and charging are both important to do on a regular basis. In general, for crystals you don't use often, charging them every week or two is a good idea. Charge and cleanse crystals when bringing them home for the first time, if they have been packed away or shelved, and after you have used them, whether for a ritual, meditation, or healing.

Sunlight is wonderful for both energetically cleansing and charging your crystals. Half an hour in the sunlight is recommended to cleanse and charge them. Just as the sun is associated with masculine, or giving, energies, and the moon is associated with feminine, or receptive, energies, the moon's magnetic pull draws energy toward it, while the sun gives off its powerful illumination. Bright sunlight delivers 111,000 lux, while the moon reflects 0.05 to 0.1 lux of sunlight, depending on its phase, making charging in sunlight a powerful method.

Other common methods of energetic cleansing involve placing crystals in earth, water, saltwater, dry salt, and the use of smoke cleansing, reiki, and sound. If using salt or saltwater, discard it when done, as it absorbs negative energies. When using sound, the bells, tuning fork, chimes, or singing bowl should release a frequency that is higher than that of the crystal in order to be effective. This is by no means an exhaustive list, as there are many methods from a variety of belief systems.

Because selenite has such a high vibration, it can be used to charge other crystals. But don't get it wet, as it can dissolve in water. Calcite, desert rose, malachite, fluorite, halite, and labradorite should also be kept away from water. Pink and purple crystals may fade with prolonged exposure to sunlight, but should be fine in sun exposure for half an hour at a time.

Spells & Rituals
An Abundance Talisman

Create an abundance-drawing talisman that you can take with you wherever you go or keep somewhere that is meaningful to you. Best performed on a Sunday or Thursday during a waxing moon.

What You Need:
Goldenrod (for prosperity and abundance)
Chamomile (for abundance)
Cinnamon (for success)
Nutmeg (for prosperity and luck)
Vervain (for money and prosperity)
Dill (for money and good fortune)
One bay leaf (for prosperity)
Chili powder (for a magical boost)
Eight Chinese good luck coins (optional)
A gold or green drawstring pouch
Sea salt
Cinnamon or clove incense
One gold or green candle
Saltwater

This potent herb and spice pouch is a powerful talisman that can be placed anywhere of significance to you, such as in a wallet or bag, on your altar if you have one, or under your pillow. Or, you may want to place it in the corresponding ba gua of your home (see appendix C for the locations).

You can buy a drawstring pouch or make it yourself. Sewing it yourself is recommended, as it gives you the advantage of infusing every stitch with your intention and thereby adding more potency to your talisman.

Before beginning, ground (see appendix A for a full grounding meditation), center, and focus on your intention. Call on your high-vibrational allies as you normally would. Empower each ingredient individually before adding it to the bag by holding it in your hands and sending it gratitude for contributing its properties to assist you, adding ingredients one at a time. Once the pouch is filled with all of the ingredients, tie the drawstring, knotting it three times. Each time you tie a knot, say: *This powerful talisman brings me abundance. This powerful talisman brings me prosperity. This powerful talisman brings me wealth.* Depending on what area of abundance you are looking to call to you, you can tailor the wording as needed as you tie the knots and incant the below.

Set the pouch in the sea salt and say three times: *I consecrate this talisman in earth. It brings me abundance, prosperity, wealth, and good fortune.*

Light the incense and pass the pouch through the smoke, saying three times: *I consecrate this talisman in air. It brings me abundance, prosperity, wealth, and good fortune.*

Light the candle and pass the pouch over the flame, saying three times: *I consecrate this talisman in fire. It brings me abundance, prosperity, wealth, and good fortune.*

Sprinkle the pouch three times with the saltwater and say three times: *I consecrate this talisman in water. It brings me abundance, prosperity, wealth, and good fortune.*

You may wish to meditate a bit while holding your talisman, further infusing it with your intention before thanking your allies and closing. It is recommended to periodically recharge the talisman. You can do this by repeating the steps above to consecrate it in each of the four elements, or by simply meditating with it and reinfusing it with your intention.

Expand Your Capacity for Wealth: A Magical Infusion

Create an infusion that blends the abundance-drawing energies of natural ingredients, Gaia's gifts to us. Best performed on a Sunday or Thursday during a waxing moon.

What You Need:
Juniper (for prosperity)
Clove (for wealth)
Mint (to increase money)
Allspice (for prosperity and increasing energy)
Grapeseed oil
Spoon
Two jars with lids
Waxed paper
Brown paper bag or opaque cloth
Muslin cloth
Wire strainer or funnel
Dark-colored glass vials or eyedroppers
Vitamin E oil

This solar-infused magical oil is perfect for dressing candles used for increasing money and expanding wealth and can be applied in a variety of uses. At various stages throughout this process, you can infuse the mixture with your intent by simply holding the jar and sending your intention into it.

Before beginning, make sure the jars and the spoon are dry and sterilized. Place the juniper, clove, mint, and allspice in a jar, leaving one to three inches of space over the mixture to cover with oil. Fill the jar, covering the mixture with room-temperature grapeseed oil. Insert the spoon handle into the jar, slowly moving it around the edges to remove air bubbles (air can cause the mixture to spoil). Place a piece of waxed paper over the top of the jar, then seal tightly with a lid. Roll the jar back and forth to ensure the ingredients are completely mixed.

Wrap the jar in an opaque cloth or place it in a brown paper bag, and leave it in a sunny area, such as a windowsill, for one to two weeks. Roll the jar again every one to three days to mix the contents. Once the time is up, the mixture is ready to strain. This can be accomplished by placing a muslin-lined funnel or muslin-lined wire strainer over a dry, sterilized jar. Gently decant the mixture into the muslin, allowing as much of the mixture as possible to drain from the jar used for the infusion.

When the jar is fully emptied into the muslin, gather up the cloth and squeeze as much of the oil as possible into the funnel or strainer. Cover the jar with the lid and seal tightly, then place it in a cool, dark place to settle overnight. Any solids remaining from the mixture will settle to the bottom of the jar, and you can strain it again through a coffee filter to fully remove the sediment.

After this process is done, pour the oil into dry, sterilized eyedroppers or vials, and add a few drops of vitamin E oil to each container to slow the oxidation process; the mixture can last up to two years with the vitamin E added. Store the oil at room temperature in a cool, dark place, as sunlight speeds oxidation.

Releasing What Does Not Serve

Use this ritual to clear stuck, stagnant, and trapped energies, to assist you in moving away from less-than-desirable situations, and to create a strong boundary of protection around you as you visualize the better situation you are moving into. Best performed on a Saturday during a waning moon or dark moon.

What You Need:

Cedar for smudging and something to place it on
Black tourmaline, cleansed and charged (see page 45)

Rosemary (for purification and new beginnings)
A cauldron or other firesafe vessel to burn the rosemary in
Amethyst and/or citrine, cleansed and charged (see page 45)
Your significator card
Six of Swords

Before beginning, ground (see appendix A for a full grounding meditation) and call in any high-vibrational divine allies you wish to assist you, focusing your mind on your intention. Place your significator card and the Six of Swords next to each other in front of the cauldron. Light the cedar and hold it in your dominant hand, facing north. Turn slowly, three times clockwise, extending the cedar at arm's length in front of you while saying three times, once with each rotation: *I cleanse and purify the space around me. I cleanse and purify my energetic field. I send all clearing energies into the earth for transmutation. I call in high-vibrational frequencies to surround and protect me.* Place the cedar aside and allow it to burn, until it extinguishes on its own, as you continue.

Hold the black tourmaline for a moment and feel its energy. Say: *I clear, release, and transmute all energy that does not serve my highest good. My boundaries are strong and secure, and I am safe at all times.* Say this three times, and feel the release as it happens, visualizing the clearing energy being sent from within you, from your crown to your feet and into the earth for transmutation, then visualizing the energy that does not serve you clearing from your aura and releasing into the earth. Visualize this happening until it is complete. Immediately envision a protective boundary around you in golden light (golden light carries a high-vibrational frequency). Intend that this sphere of golden light remains in place at all times and that it cannot be dismantled, degraded, or interfered with in any way. It helps if you reinforce this sphere daily with intention and visualization. Send gratitude to the black tourmaline and place it over your significator card.

Place as much rosemary in the cauldron as you like, and light it. As it burns, hold the amethyst and/or citrine and feel gratitude for its assistance. The amethyst will send you healing energies and assists with releasing and clearing what has left you; it also dissolves negativity. Citrine also clears negative energy and brings you high-vibrational light, confidence, and empowerment. If you are using both citrine and amethyst, meditate with each for a little while as the rosemary burns, and relax, allowing the process to unfold. Visualize yourself moving, energetically and otherwise, away from what you have released and into a new, better situation. Embody this new mindset completely, never wavering from it and maintaining your focus with clarity.

When you are ready, move the black tourmaline next to the tarot cards and place the Six of Swords over your significator, then place the crystals on the cards. Send gratitude to your higher self and to the divine allies who are supporting you.

Healing a Compromised Aura

Use this ritual to quickly seal any rips or tears in your aura. Best performed on a Sunday or Thursday during a waxing or full moon.

What You Need:

Pyrite, cleansed and charged (see page 45)

This simple yet effective ritual can repair any rips, holes, tears, or shreds in your aura and restores an aura that has been in any way compromised. This ritual is useful if you feel you need additional protection and if unwanted energies have been affecting you.

Crystals hold potent energy that can assist us whenever we are in need. Pyrite is known as an abundance-bringing mineral, but this powerful stone of protection also has the remarkable ability to seal your aura if it has been compromised. An aura can be compromised in a variety of different ways, but the most critical step once you feel you are affected is to seal it up. Your aura is an extension of who you are and acts as a field of protection around you. If it is compromised, it can let in all sorts of unwanted energies.

Start by creating a circle of protection around you (see appendix B) and calling on your high-vibrational allies. Ground your energy (see appendix A for a full grounding meditation) and give thanks to Gaia for the crystal she has provided for your use. Send her your gratitude as you hold the pyrite in front of your solar plexus and feel the pyrite's energy enter you through your chakra. You may feel an energy wrap itself around you like a warm blanket, or it may feel like you are being coated in a layer of protection that fills in your aura and creates a seal around you. This may feel like liquid light and can surround you quickly all at once or may happen slowly. Hold the pyrite in front of your solar plexus for as long as you feel its energy entering your field. Simply relax in gratitude and allow this to happen.

When you feel the process is complete, send love and gratitude to the crystal for its healing and assistance, and to your allies for their support. Ground your energy and close the circle. Be sure to cleanse and charge the pyrite before its next use.

Chapter 3

MARCH: THE WORM MOON

March's full moon is named for the earthworms that begin to make their appearance at winter's end. Other names for this moon are the Storm Moon, the Sugar Moon, the Crow Moon, the Crust Moon, and the Sap Moon.

The Worm Moon tarot spreads included in this chapter examine how to prepare for upcoming growth, what seeds are ready to be planted, what will soon be emerging, where there is current growth, how to support that growth, and opportunities for expansion and ascension.

The spells and rituals in this chapter include surrounding yourself with love and connecting to your higher self, planting new seeds, and creating energetic expansion to make way for growth in certain areas of life.

Moon Phase Cards as Indicators of Timing

Some tarot decks include moon indicator cards—representing the new or dark moon, full moon, half moon, and quarter moon phases. There are also entire decks dedicated to representing the moon phases. Moon cards (sometimes called Luna cards) are especially helpful to give you an idea of timing when you are doing a reading. For example, if you drew the Fool and the full moon card, this could indicate something new beginning around the full moon.

If you have a deck that includes moon phase cards, simply including them in your regular deck and allowing them to emerge naturally in a reading can be useful in shaping a timeline for you; or, you may want to set them aside to draw from intentionally. If you have a deck of moon phase cards, you can use these to complement your readings or simply ask a question about timing and draw from the deck. Some moon phase decks have as few as eight cards, while others include twenty-eight cards representing the moon phases. Which deck you use depends on how specific you want to be in your readings, and on what resonates with you.

Spreads

Preparing Foundations for Growth

When the frozen world begins to thaw, it allows the worms to move through the earth beneath our feet. Their important work prepares the soil for new life to spring forth by aerating it, enhancing its structure, and reintroducing nutrients that bring fertility. Use this spread (see illustration 3-1) to call attention to areas of your life where your foundations would benefit from restructuring and to uncover how to prepare yourself for what is developing.

Suggested questions:

1. What lies ahead for me?
2. What can I do to prepare for it?
3. What in my life needs restructuring?
4. Where else does change need to take place?
5. How can I fortify my foundations?
6. What is currently working for me that I can use?
7. What future growth needs tending?
8. How can I ensure its greatest success?
9. What can I do to further prepare myself?
10. A message from Gaia.

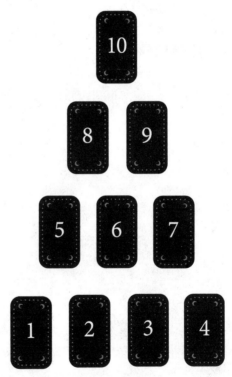

Illustration 3-1: Preparing Foundations
for Growth

The Significance of Numbers

If you notice the same number or numeric sequence seemingly everywhere you look, it's likely you're spotting evidence of the universe in communication with you (see the introduction for a chart to help demystify the essential meanings of the numbers zero through nine). Sometimes, your attention will simply be drawn in a certain direction, as if your higher self or your guides are saying, *Look at this*. Pay attention to what catches your eye and what you are drawn to—this could be receipts, license plates, the time, and other numbers you encounter throughout the day.

You might also notice numbers repeating on tarot cards in a reading. Maybe several fours appear in your spread, for example. Looking into the significance of the number four could be beneficial to you and reveal another layer of meaning that you can apply to your life in some way. As you consider the correspondences of the numbers and what the suits represent, observe any meanings that jump out at you or resonate with you in some way. If this happens, the message is probably meant for you.

You can also ask the cards to reveal a number that is relevant to you. Simply sit with this intention and draw a card from the deck. If you draw a pip card, the suit it is from indicates to what area of your life the number applies. For example, if you draw the Four of Pentacles, fours can represent stability and pentacles have to do with earthly concerns and material matters.

Where the minor arcana cards (the numbered pip cards ace through ten, plus the four court cards) relate to everyday concerns that are generally passing through our lives and are less permanent, the major arcana cards reflect more overarching themes that can be related to karma and life lessons. So, drawing the four in the major arcana, the Emperor, has a different influence than the Four of Pentacles. Rather than representing material stability, continuing with the previous example, it could indicate the need for a deeper, more foundational source of stability in your life, or it could be telling you that one is on its way. To gain further clarity on the card you draw, continue with a line of questioning, tarot deck at the ready.

Sowing Seeds

Mother Nature teaches us the importance of timing, and of patience. Just as you would not expect to get immediate results from seeds you planted at the beginning of the season, the timing and the conditions in which you plant seeds in your own life is significant. This spread (see illustration 3-2) can help you to gain clarity on what is ready for you to begin focusing your efforts and your attention on, and what you are ready to begin.

Suggested questions:

1. What seeds are ready to be planted in my life?
2. What am I ready for now?
3. Where would it be beneficial for me to focus my efforts at this time?
4. What can I do to prepare?
5. How should I nurture this?
6. How can I ensure the best outcome?
7. What should I do to see this through to fruition?
8. Advice from Gaia.

Illustration 3-2: Sowing Seeds

What Is Preparing to Emerge

There are times when we sense that something is about to happen, that there is something shifting in our lives that we can't quite put a finger on—something that we catch a momentary glimpse of that is just too fleeting to process. Use this spread (see illustration 3-3) to reveal what is about to change or what is getting ready to emerge in your life.

Suggested questions:

1. What is shifting for me now?
2. What is preparing to emerge for me?
3. What area(s) of my life will this impact?
4. What changes will this bring about?
5. How can I prepare for these changes?
6. What else should I know about this?

Illustration 3-3: What Is Preparing to Emerge

The Importance of Rituals

Regardless of how you came to the practice of rituals, there is one primary motivator behind this work: to create change. Sometimes, of course, we may simply wish to honor our allies, to connect with them, or to sit in meditation—not setting out overtly to create any change. However, gratitude, connection, and quieting the mind can create change in our lives and within us on profoundly deep and far-reaching levels.

By nature, inherently, we are born creators, creators of our own realities and change-makers through our thoughts, actions, and beliefs. Rituals and spells serve as methods of focus in which we direct our will and intention using tools like candles, crystals, or meditation to create some desired change or outcome.

This work is one way of "getting ahead of it," as Abraham-Hicks would say (Hicks, 2004). We set forth a desired outcome before it happens, and then take steps to ensure it reaches that state. We can plan for it, or visualize it, or create vision boards about it, or daydream its happy conclusion, or light a candle and meditate on it, or create a charm bag and carry it with us. All are means to the same end—that is, shaping our own reality.

Sprouts Unfurling

This spread (see illustration 3-4) allows you to take a look at what is currently growing in your life, to examine those tender sprouts that are newly emerging and making their way into your reality. That first emergence is a fragile time when something either grows and thrives, or recedes, returning to the earth to offer its nutrients back to the soil.

Suggested questions:

1. What is newly emerging for me?
2. Why is it emerging now?
3. What energies are feeding it?
4. How can I nurture it?
5. How can I best support its future growth?
6. How is it supporting me?
7. What is it here to teach me?
8. How can it help me to grow?
9. What changes will it bring about?
10. What is the greatest possibility it can mature into?

Illustration 3-4: Sprouts Unfurling

Tending Your Garden

Every gardener understands the importance of tending their garden—pulling weeds, tilling the soil and fertilizing it, trimming and pruning when necessary. Use this spread (see illustration 3-5) to gain clarity on how best to tend your own spiritual garden and to shine a light on what would benefit from your loving care and attention.

Suggested questions:

1. What is the state of my spiritual garden?

2. What card best represents my current emotional state?

3. What needs nourishment?

4. What needs pruning?

5. What weeds are present in my garden?

6. What seeds are beginning to sprout?

7. What seeds should I sow now?

8. What requires my immediate attention?

9. What requires my ongoing attention?

10. What would benefit from my loving care?

Illustration 3-5: Tending Your Garden

Choosing What to Write With

Whether you are writing something by hand for a spell or in a journal, consider the importance of the writing instrument. Pencil can easily smudge and be erased; it is, by nature, impermanent. Ink, on the other hand, has longevity and, unless you are using erasable ink, it is permanent. Ink also makes a stronger physical impact, as it tends to be bolder than graphite and seeps deeply into the paper.

The color of ink you choose also matters, especially in rituals. Consider the meaning and associations of colors (see the color correspondences chart in the introduction). If you are writing abundance affirmations, green or gold ink would be great choices. Or, something written to encourage psychic awareness and expansion could be written in purple, for example.

The physical act of writing by hand also carries significance. There is a certain weight and intention directed from the physical body into the writing instrument that shapes the words written by your hand on paper that is so direct and infused with your personal energy and vibration. Typing on a computer keyboard is more ephemeral than writing by hand and does not carry quite the same energetic impact, but many prefer it for channeling and automatic writing, as it allows for a quicker transcription.

The Abundant Vine

The vine represents endurance, tenacity, and strength, and can be a source of abundance, bearing fruit for all to enjoy. The Druids are thought to have seen the vine as a symbol of fertility, connection, opportunity, and expansion. Because it is a climbing plant, the vine, in a physical sense, seeks ever-greater heights. This spread (see illustration 3-6) takes a look at where you are ascending in your life, where there are new opportunities for connection, and where you are expanding on a spiritual level.

Suggested questions:

1. A card representing where I am spiritually.
2. In what ways am I currently expanding?
3. Where am I ready to start expanding?
4. What new opportunities are available to me now?
5. What new opportunities can I cultivate?
6. What new connections are available to me?
7. What current connections can I use to elevate myself?
8. What new heights am I ascending to?
9. What can I do to ensure my best success?
10. A message from Gaia.

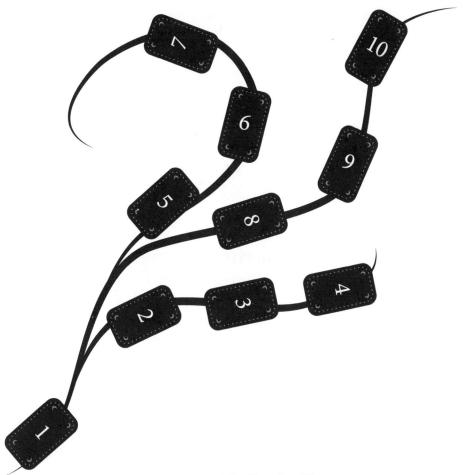

Illustration 3-6: The Abundant Vine

The Manifestation Journal

Keeping a manifestation journal is a good way to record any signs, synchronicities, mantras, musings, affirmations, wishes, hopes and dreams, notes of gratitude, and anything relevant to your manifestation journey. So much insight can be gained from looking back on things you might otherwise have forgotten and following the winding trail (or sometimes, the beeline) from the initial thought to its physical, manifested form. Writing something down also empowers it, because the act of writing and the written word carry power. A manifestation journal is a fantastic forum in which to inscribe anything you want to dream into being.

Spells & Rituals

I Wrap the Warm Blanket of Love Around Me

This ritual allows you to tap into self-love and align with your inner being, or higher self. Best performed on a Friday during a new or waxing moon.

What You Need:

One pink candle

Rose incense

Rose quartz, cleansed and charged (see page 45)

Prepare the candle by cleansing it in whichever way you prefer—simply doing this with intention is fine. Bless the candle and set the intention, while holding it, that it brings you into alignment with your inner being and your highest form of self-love.

Begin by grounding (see appendix A for a full grounding meditation) and calling on high-vibrational allies to assist you. Your divine support team is always ready and willing to help at any moment; all you have to do is call on them. You can simply ask for the assistance and support of any high-vibrational allies who are appropriate for this ritual if you do not have any specific ones in mind.

Light the incense and thank the allies who are present working with you and assisting you. Thank your inner being, your higher self, whom you can invite now to be more present in your field. Sit for a moment, holding the rose quartz as you quiet your mind and focus on releasing resistance.

Feel your burdens lift as you embrace the well-being that flows to you constantly, in an endless abundance of pure Source energy. You may see this as a stream entering into your crown chakra and filling you with high-vibrational light, an ascension column of light surrounding you, or golden light expanding outward from your heart chakra to surround you past the outer layer of your aura in a protective sphere. Feel all heaviness, worries, fears, and concerns begin to dissipate. Imagine this as a physical weight lifting from your shoulders and from your entire body as you begin to feel lighter and lighter. The more burdens and heaviness you release, the more light can enter.

When you are ready, light the candle and say:

It is my intention to come into full alignment with my inner being. I surrender now in the safety of this space and ask my inner being to be more present within me.

From my crown chakra, my inner being expands my enlightenment and wisdom and my connection to the divine.

From my third eye, my inner being allows me to see through to the truth of every matter and strengthens my connection to my intuition.

From my throat chakra, my inner being helps me to speak my truth and communicate with clarity.

From my heart chakra, my inner being connects me to my authenticity and helps me to embody my highest truth.

From my solar plexus, my inner being strengthens my connection to my power and allows me to expand in courage, confidence, and in the knowing of who I truly am.

From my sacral chakra, my inner being brings me expressive creativity and healthy, balanced relationships.

From my root chakra, my inner being helps me to feel secure, grounded, and connected to strong foundations and my divine support system.

Surrender into the knowing that you are safe. You may feel a pressure on your head as your inner being descends further into your body. Simply let go in gratitude, breathe deeply, and allow this to happen.

Say:

I invite healing to me now. I welcome healing to surround me on every layer and level of my being and existence, across all times, dimensions, space, and realities.

Sit and allow this healing to happen. You may feel physical warmth around you. The more you surrender and allow the process to happen, the more fully it can take place, and on deeper levels.

Let the candle flame become a focal point as you close your eyes in meditation. Envision the light of the flame with your eyes closed and imagine it expanding and filling you, surrounding you with pink light. Say:

I wrap the warm blanket of high-vibrational love around me. I invite the highest divine love to fill me and surround me. I invite this love into my heart. I invite this love into my mind. I am surrounded by divine love. I emanate divine love and warmth. I am strengthened in the highest energies of divine peace, truth, and protection. I project love in all that I do and say. I am loved and supported.

Bask in the glow of the pink light and envision it as a sphere of pure, divine love surrounding you. Feel it as it enters your heart center. When you are done, thank your inner being and send love to all allies who assisted you, grounding and closing in gratitude.

Planting New Seeds

Use this ritual to plant new seeds of intention. Best performed on a Tuesday or Thursday during a new or waxing moon.

What You Need:
One green candle
A piece of paper
A pen
A cauldron or other firesafe vessel

After using the spreads in this chapter to gain clarity on the new beginnings and opportunities that are ready to enter your life, ground (see appendix A for a full grounding meditation) and center in your intention. Visualize the new beginnings you are setting forth without getting bogged down in the details of how it will happen or the steps you will take to reach its successful conclusion; the most effective method is to visualize only the happy outcome, yourself living the end result, and release all details to the universe. Otherwise, you could get caught up in doubt and disbelief and assign too many specifics, therefore limiting your outcome.

Cleanse the candle with saltwater, then charge it with your intention and light it. Write only your desired outcome in clear wording on the paper, then hold it in front of the candle and read it aloud. Fold the paper so that it will fit in the cauldron while burning, then light it in the flame and drop it in the cauldron. Be sure to do this in an area where it is safe to burn the paper. Know that, as your directive is burning, the fire is releasing its power to the universe to be realized and made manifest.

After the paper has completely burned, bury the ashes outside. Visualize the happy outcome on a regular basis and rest easily in the knowing that it will happen.

Growth and Expansion

This spell can be used as an all-purpose catalyst that increases your influence and the impact you make in your life. Best performed on a Thursday during a full or waxing moon.

What You Need:
One green candle
One purple candle
A cedar smudging stick
The Wheel of Fortune card
Your significator card

Jupiter is associated with expansion, and Thursday is his day. The number that corresponds with Jupiter is four, so if you were to begin this spell at 4:00 or, better yet, 4:44, it would further strengthen your work. Begin by grounding (see appendix A for a full grounding meditation) and casting a circle of protection (see appendix B).

Place the Wheel of Fortune card over your significator in front of the candles. Light the cedar and cleanse each candle in its smoke to purify them of unwanted energies and energies that do not serve your intentions. Circle your workspace clockwise three times, holding the cedar in your dominant hand at arm's length. Each time you circle, expand the circumference so the circle becomes larger with every rotation, but do not allow the outer circle to go outside of the circle of protection you have already cast. As you do this, say with each rotation: *I call upon Jupiter to help me expand in these areas of my life* (name them specifically).

Etch the Jupiter symbol into each candle using the carving tool of your choice. As you carve, recite your intention over the candles to infuse them with the energy.

Light the green candle and say:

My energy is expanding. My impact is expanding. My influence is expanding. My wealth is expanding. My abilities are expanding. My knowledge is expanding. All is in accordance with my highest good. Thank you, Jupiter, for assisting me in this expansion.

You can add to this or adjust the wording according to what you are looking to expand in your life. Then light the purple candle and repeat the incantation.

Standing (or sitting) in front of the candles, visualize what you want to expand increasing to reach your desired outcome or state of being. See it in as much detail as possible. Hear the congratulations, shake the hands that are offered to you, and really put yourself in the desired situation as much as possible to solidify your intentions. This visualization is one you can keep coming back to, either adding more detail to it or repeating your chosen outcome until it manifests in your physical reality.

When you are ready, give gratitude to Jupiter, thank any other allies who assisted you, ground your energy, and close the circle.

Chapter 4
APRIL: THE PINK MOON

April's cheerfully named Pink Moon hearkens to the blush-colored phlox that makes its debut during this time of early spring. This moon is sometimes called the Egg Moon, Growing Moon, Fish Moon, or Sprouting Grass Moon.

The Pink Moon tarot spreads included in this chapter help you to tune in to your internal guidance system, gain clarity on your state of alignment, reflect on the positive aspects of your life, reveal where you shine the brightest, and discover where you could be more loving to yourself and to those around you.

The spells and rituals in this chapter include drawing the perfect partner to you, summoning happiness, and connecting to your light for empowerment and expansion.

Connecting to Your Higher Self

We each have a higher self, a high-vibrational being of which only a small part dwells within the physical body. As an extension or physical manifestation of this divine being, you can close the gap between you and your higher self by raising your vibration. This allows you to receive guidance and wisdom from a being whose perspective is much broader—a being who has all of your best interests at heart and who holds in its attention the powerful knowing of the well-being of which you are capable.

Meditation is an excellent way to raise your vibration. Sitting comfortably for twenty minutes at a time is recommended. Some find it helpful to focus on a steady sound or white noise, such as an air conditioner, to silence the mental chatter. When you quiet the mind, you stop any thoughts that are holding you back or causing you worry, anxiety, or stress. This allows you to shift your vibration by releasing what normally separates you from your higher self, whether that is negative thinking or thoughts focused on the physical realm that are blocking you from receiving higher wisdom.

Entering the meditative space with an open mind ensures that you are open to guidance from the higher realms. After a while of sitting in the mental space of no-thought, you may receive an image or idea. It may not seem like much; it could simply be an urge to call someone or visit a certain place or pull something out of storage. The idea may arrive as soft encouragement, or it could feel like an irresistible impulse, like the best idea you've ever had. But when the idea or thought comes to you, even if it doesn't make logical sense, following through could lead you to a sequence of events where the end result just might be one of the manifestations you've been working toward.

Your higher self is always ready to guide you, and is waiting for you to be in a receptive space so you can receive the thought or idea or impulse that will lead you to the manifestation of your desires. Tuning in to your internal wisdom and trusting your intuition can lead you down a trail that ends with a physical, tangible manifestation, or it can bring you valuable understanding and wisdom that, for example, helps you to heal in some way, perhaps by showing you how to release and clear blocks, old energies, or ways of thinking that no longer serve you. Once those are gone, manifestation can happen with more ease.

Spreads

Tuning In to Your Internal Guidance

Tuning in to your intuition can sometimes feel mystifying, especially if you were raised in a society or culture that prioritizes logic, reason, and rational knowledge. How do you know what is your intuition versus your logical, rational mind? The word *intuition* comes from the Latin *intueri* and denotes an inner knowing that surpasses logic. Intuition often comes from feeling, rather than thinking; you *feel* like you should do something without knowing why.

Like instinct, your intuition can help you to know or comprehend something right away. Instinct is a knowing—knowing without knowing how or why, you just simply know. The word *instinct* comes from the Latin for *impulse.* So, tuning in to your internal guidance system can mean tuning in to your feeling about something, or following an impulse that feels right instead of rationalizing your way out of it or questioning or doubting it. Use this spread (see illustration 4-1) to help you gain clarity on how to better attune to your inner guidance.

Suggested questions:

1. What is holding me back from receiving guidance?

2. Where am I blocking my intuition?

3. How can I better attune to my own intuition?

4. How can I better trust my instincts?

5. How can I strengthen the connection to my higher self?

6. What is my intuition trying to tell me now?

7. A message from my higher self.

Illustration 4-1: Tuning In to Your
Internal Guidance

Coming into Alignment

Your internal guidance system—your emotions—let you know when you are in alignment with your inner being. When you are in alignment, you feel happy, positive, and filled with clarity. Things like worry, doubt, fear, and reliving the past can cause you to be out of alignment by introducing resistance and activating those energies in your vibration—and attracting more of the same. Abraham-Hicks teaches that you can't fix the past by worrying about it and you can't release resistance by focusing on what is causing it.

You can always come back into alignment, regardless of your vibrational starting point, by redirecting your thoughts toward increasingly more positive ones, like climbing a staircase one step at a time. Because the law of attraction attracts or brings you whatever you think about, without making any distinction between whether you want it or not, it always benefits you to think about what you want. This spread (see illustration 4-2) can help you gain clarity on anything that is hindering you from reaching an aligned state.

Suggested questions:

1. Where am I out of alignment?

2. Where am I holding on to resistance?

3. What is blocking me?

4. How can I let go of it?

5. What can I do to restore my balance?

6. What is the best way for me to come into alignment?

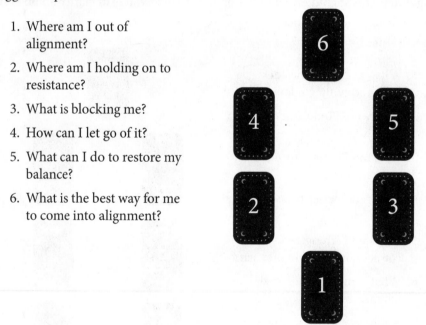

Illustration 4-2: Coming into Alignment

We Live in an Abundant Universe

Some fear that opening themselves up to receive guidance through meditation will let in unwanted energies or beings. Because of the law of attraction, you get whatever you think about and whatever you hold to be true. If you enter a meditative space with an open heart and mind and connect to the peace and well-being that is all around you, knowing that you are safe, loved, and protected, your experience will be positive.

But if you enter with beliefs that contradict that with fear or anxiety, for example, you are blocking yourself from receiving the valuable guidance that is available to you and attracting energies you don't want. If you find this to be the case for you, it can be helpful to start by visualizing a sphere of high-vibrational, golden-white light all around you (see appendix A for the full grounding and protection meditation). Once you find a calm, peaceful center and feel the ease and well-being within, you can better relax into the meditation and will ultimately have a more rewarding experience.

Positivity Abounds

Reasons to feel joy are everywhere, if you only look for them. What makes you happy? What brings you pleasure? What relationships in your life make you light up? What music makes you want to get up and dance? You've heard that laughter is the best medicine, and medical professionals know that patients with a positive attitude heal faster. Everyone deserves to feel joy, and happiness has a powerful impact on both mind and body. Use this spread (see illustration 4-3) to reveal ways you can allow more happiness to flow to you.

Suggested questions:

1. What opportunities are there for me to bring more positivity into my life?
2. How can I be more positive in my thinking?
3. What benefits will thinking positively have on my life?
4. What could use my positive attention right now?
5. What positive situations are currently developing for me?
6. How can I let more positivity into my life overall?

Illustration 4-3: Positivity Abounds

SHINING YOUR BRIGHTEST

Anytime you doubt yourself or feel less-than in any way, think about what your inner being would say to you. Considering who you are—a divine being of pure Source energy—can be a powerful reminder. Remembering that you are part of a pure, generative, force of positive energy tells you that you are a powerful creator of your own reality, that you can manifest anything you want, live any life you want, and be whoever you choose to be.

You shine your brightest when you believe in yourself, when you trust in your own abilities and potential. You may not know everything there is to know about something or feel like you're good at it, but what is most important is that it brings you joy. You are always learning and growing and you always have the ability to continue expanding into the best version of yourself. We are all born with a blank slate. What we write on that slate is up to us.

Where You Shine

As you move through life, you may feel appreciated or unappreciated to varying degrees. When others feel jealous or are reacting from their own wounds, they may try to diminish your positive attributes in some way. There are many things that can cause you to lose sight of your best qualities, your talents, and your gifts. Or, you may not realize how good you are at something or the potential it has to develop into an outcome that is powerfully beneficial to you. Use this spread (see illustration 4-4) to shed light on your best aspects.

Suggested questions:

1. What are my greatest gifts?
2. What are my core strengths?
3. What are my best qualities?
4. In what ways do I bring happiness to others?
5. How can I shine my light more brightly?
6. What are my hidden qualities that have not yet come to light?
7. How can I bring them forward?
8. In what ways can I most fruitfully apply them in my life?
9. Where would it benefit me to shine my light at this time?
10. Wisdom from my inner being.

Illustration 4-4: Where You Shine

Tuning In to the Heart

Perhaps more songs have been written about love than about any other subject. It's no secret that love is a powerful force in the universe—some would say it is the most power-ful. Whether you are seeking guidance on self-love or on your relationships with others, this spread (see illustration 4-5) can help you uncover the nuances of those often-complex emotional landscapes and help you sort out how best to move ahead in a way that benefits all involved.

Suggested questions:

1. Where can I be more loving?
2. What is holding me back?
3. What is the best way for me to address what's holding me back?
4. What relationship would benefit from my loving attention right now?
5. What action should I take in regards to that relationship?
6. What would most benefit that relationship overall?
7. How can I be more loving to myself?
8. How can I expand the love in my life?
9. What does my heart need right now?
10. A message from my heart.

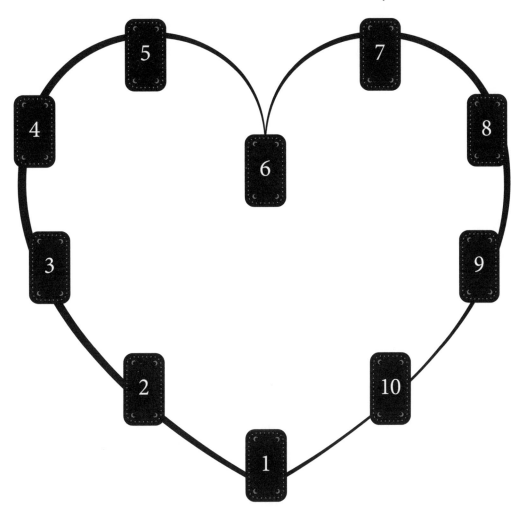

Illustration 4-5: Tuning In to the Heart

Spells & Rituals

Drawing the Perfect Partner

Use this ritual to attract the perfect partner for you. Best performed on a Friday during a new or waxing moon.

What You Need:
The Lovers card
The Two of Cups
Saltwater
One red candle
One pink candle
Rose incense
Red and/or pink rose petals
Image or statue of Venus or Aphrodite
Tool for carving into the candles
Paper and a red pen
One length of red ribbon
One length of pink ribbon

This spell can be performed on the new moon or during the several days following it. Before beginning, prepare yourself by taking a cleansing bath in saltwater with red and/or pink rose petals sprinkled on the water; you will also need to set aside some of the petals for the ritual. As you soak, visualize the energies of past romantic connections (and love interests) dissolving from your field, as all cords of attachment dissipate and you visualize cutting the ties that bind you to them, and them to you. Soak until you feel these have dissolved completely.

After the bath, dress in something that makes you feel romantic. Cleanse each candle with saltwater, then arrange the tarot cards, goddess image or statue, rose petals, and candles in any way you like. Light the incense and meditate on the tarot cards until you feel their symbolism has entered your vibration. Carve symbols of love into each candle—this could be hearts or any other symbol that is meaningful to you; you might wish to carve your name into one and "perfect partner" into the other. As you light each candle, infuse them with your intention; this could be to bring the one who is right for you into your life, to bring you someone who will make you happy, or whatever it is you desire. Be sure to intend that the partnership is in alignment with the highest good for both of you. Ethics are important: it is strongly recommended never to attempt to manipulate the energies of another or impose upon their free will, not to mention that partnerships are so much more rewarding when they are based on authentic, mutually shared connections.

On the paper, write a description of your perfect partner, then roll it into a scroll and tie it with the ribbons. Place the scroll between the two tarot cards. As the candles burn down, feel yourself being wrapped in high-vibrational love, visualizing a pink light around you as you meditate on how you would feel around your ideal partner. Visualize yourself laughing and having fun with this person, and doing all the things you might do together. You can leave the scroll between the tarot cards and infuse it again with a visualization every Friday, if you wish, until your intentions manifest.

Summoning Happiness

Shift your mindset to become a magnet for happiness. Best performed on a Sunday or Thursday during a waxing or full moon.

What You Need:
The Sun card
Your significator card
Clove incense
One yellow candle
Small glass of water (that you will drink)
Citrine, cleansed and purified (see page 45)

Happiness is a mindset. By choosing to be happy, you are taking control of your emotional state of mind, and by extension, your state of being. This spell supports and reinforces your choice to be happy, as you choose to be grateful for what you have, rather than focusing on the negative. As you focus on what you are grateful for, you shift your energy to draw more of that to you.

Begin by placing your significator card next the the Sun card. Light the incense and cleanse the candle in the smoke. As you light the candle, infuse it with the intention to amplify your happiness, joy, and gratitude. Position the glass of water so the candle flame is reflected into it and it is close to the cards. Water absorbs the vibration of anything that is near it, so your happiness-infused candle is imprinting its vibrations onto the water.

Meditate while holding the citrine for as long as you wish, thanking the crystal for its assistance and feeling its effects. Citrine dispels negative emotion and brings mental and emotional balance and clarity of mind. As you hold it, you may begin to feel your energy shift or feel sensations around your crown chakra. Allow the energy to shift and stabilize until the process is complete.

Place the Sun card over your significator card and say:

I choose happiness. I choose gratitude. I have the ability to be happy in every situation. I am in control of my emotional state. Happiness is amplified in my mind, in my life, and in my heart.

Gaze into the glass of water, focusing on the reflection of the flame, as you consciously invite this happiness mindset to settle into your vibration. When you are ready, drink the water. Feel gratitude for everything good in your life and for everything that makes you happy. Let the candle burn out on its own.

Be Your Best, Shine Your Light

Release limiting beliefs, refocus your energy, and align with your inner being. Best performed on a Sunday during a full or waxing moon, but can be done anytime.

What You Need:
A quiet space with privacy
Selenite

Setting intentions is one of the most powerful ways to create change in your reality. Supporting your intention with belief is vital for a successful outcome. This is a ritual you can come back to as often as you feel you need to, and you can change the wording of the mantras below to suit your needs and as you evolve in the process. Ensure that when you say them, you are supporting the words with the knowing that you are creating your own reality through your intentions, focus, thoughts, and beliefs.

Selenite has a pure, clarifying energy that makes it a good ally to use for clearing blockages and to shift into more positive thinking. (Interestingly, this crystallized form of gypsum is named after the Greek moon goddess, Selene.) Meditate while holding the selenite, noticing any thoughts that come up; these may indicate energies that need to be cleared. Simply acknowledge anything that arises that isn't of a positive nature and think, *I clear, release, and transmute everything that does not serve my highest good,* as you feel it leaving you. You can use this mantra anytime you catch yourself in a negative thought or memory. By clearing an unpleasant feeling or emotion, you are clearing its energy from your vibration. While you may still remember it, it won't be an active part of your vibration anymore, which means that it will no longer hold influence over you or affect your point of attraction.

Intend that, as you continue this process, you are entering more and more into a state of alignment with your highest good or higher self. Pay attention to what comes up for you as you say the above mantra. After you clear the unwanted, state your intentions for how you want to feel instead and welcome those new feelings to you. For example, you could say, *I welcome perfect peace to fill my heart.* If you have any contradictory thoughts, notice these and remember that you create your own reality by what you choose to believe and focus on. According to Abraham-Hicks, "A belief is a thought you continue to think" (Hicks, 2004). You have total control over what you choose to think; thinking something long enough causes the law of attraction to draw similar energies and components to you. If you make a daily habit of thinking something such as, *Everything gets better and better for me all the time,* and if you support this with your belief, then you will begin to see evidence of it in your life.

Continue to clear, release, and transmute the contradictory energies, feelings, and beliefs. You can spend as long as you feel you need to in this ritual, focusing and refocusing and exploring your beliefs and thoughts as they come up, questioning anything negative that arises. Your goal should be to come to a place of perfect focus that is free of doubt and conflicting energies, and to integrate that focus so that it becomes your new vibrational set point. For most people, this won't happen in a single sitting, and this ritual is one you can come back to time and again as you continue to make the necessary adjustments.

Often, simply becoming aware of a limiting belief is a way of shifting it out of your thinking; you can question it, clear it with intention, then replace it with a more positive thought or something that reflects your preferred belief. The more deadwood you clear, the more room you make for healing and positive energy to come in. And the clearer you are, the more you are able to shine your light and manifest your intentions with ease from a clear and focused point of attraction.

As you say (or think) each statement, sit with it, allowing its truth and authenticity to sink in, feeling its power transforming you:

I embrace my positive aspects and allow them to shine.
I am a divine being.
I am creating a beautiful reality.
It is good for me to shine my high-vibrational light.
I shine my light more each day.
Shining my light empowers me.
I shine my light in a way that benefits me.
I shine my light in a way that benefits others.
I shine my light in the best and most authentic ways possible.
I am improving all the time.
I am becoming better at what I do every day.
I love who I am and who I am becoming.
I am attuned to divine knowledge.
I continue to align more and more with my inner being.
I receive clarity, knowledge, and wisdom with ease.
It is easy for me to focus on the positive.
I shine brighter every day.

Chapter 5
MAY: THE FLOWER MOON

Sometimes called the Corn Planting Moon, the Hare Moon, or the Milk Moon, May's Flower Moon is named in honor of the blooms that make their appearance during this vibrant time of becoming, a time when the planting of corn heralds the certain arrival of the season of fertility.

The Flower Moon tarot spreads included in this chapter shine a light on what is beautiful and thriving in your life and all around you, guiding you to explore what can be further developed, how to navigate through change and transition, where it would be beneficial to slow down and enjoy life, and what is needing your focused attention.

The spells and rituals in this chapter include amplifying well-being, beauty, and radiance; a corn fertility spell; an abundance knot talisman; and a spell to find what is lost.

Celebrating the Beauty of Inner Wisdom

We read tarot for a multitude of reasons that vary depending on the seasons of our lives and the particular circumstances in which we find ourselves. Most often, we engage with tarot to better understand a situation or to know what happens next. It is important to remember that the cards reveal how things will unfold if a situation continues along its current path. Our beliefs, actions, and choices can powerfully affect the outcome or set things off on an entirely different course. Nothing is fixed, and change is the only constant in the universe.

Most of us have had the experience of not listening to our inner guidance then regretting it later, as it turned out to be exactly the right thing to do. As we move through life, we learn to trust ourselves more, to trust that gut instinct, even if it doesn't make sense in the moment. Trusting the wisdom of your heart is important above all. Your inner being knows you—*is* you—and has access to all information. No matter what anyone says or predicts or believes about you, your internal compass trumps all.

If you want to increase your ability to perceive your inner guidance, simply ask. Make a request of your inner being and you will be guided to your own wisdom. You will learn how to decipher the various ways the universe communicates with you and recognize that your inner being is in divine partnership with you, guiding you in ways you might not have expected.

Spreads

A Celebration of Beauty

There is always something beautiful to celebrate, even if we don't immediately see it. It could be the smile on a loved one's face or spring flowers growing in proliferation. Often, there is hidden beauty in our own lives; we may just be so focused on other things that it is obscured from our view. Use this spread (see illustration 5-1) to help you become aware of the beauty that is already in your life and where there is more available to you, ready for you to tap into.

Suggested questions:

1. What beauty can I celebrate in my life?
2. What beauty should I nurture?
3. Where is there potential for me to create more beauty?
4. What beauty am I ignoring or not seeing?
5. What are my most beautiful aspects?
6. Where am I thriving?
7. Where is there potential for me to thrive more?
8. What beauty is on the horizon for me?

Illustration 5-1: A Celebration of Beauty

Getting the Most out of Your Readings

When you are reading tarot cards, there is the possibility that you can block information coming to you. If you are upset about something or in any way feeling negative or experiencing unbalanced emotions, you can unduly influence the reading and its results. This tends to have a compounding effect; when you are feeling unsettled, scattered, or unfocused and cards arise that reflect those feelings, there is a tendency to worry even more if what the cards are showing is perceived to be some negative outcome, when really, the cards are reflecting your current vibrational state.

Remember that when you are all knotted up about something, it can't possibly come to you. Negative feelings hold it away from you by blocking it, whether that is through discomfort, irritation, impatience, or otherwise focusing on the fact that it is not in your life or does not match your desires. When you relax, you allow. In this state, not only do you open your receptivity so that the things you want can flow to you, you also let information and guidance from Source and your divine support team come through.

For those reasons, it is beneficial to you on many levels to find a way of getting into a relaxed state before pulling cards or having someone read for you. Some ways to do that are through laughter, meditation, or doing something fun or that relaxes you, such as painting or some other creative pursuit. If something is really lodged in your vibration, do whatever you can to take a step back from it and then consult the cards when you are feeling better. Sometimes it helps to write it out, talk to someone to gain perspective, sit with the situation a while and let clarity come to you, or to approach things from a broader perspective, remembering that we are eternal beings and are supported at all times with a greater love than we can fathom here on this earthly plane.

Planting the Seeds of Intention

The new moon is an especially potent time for planting the seeds of intention for whatever it is you want to see manifested in your life. There are many different ways to seed your intentions. If you are new to the practice of intention-setting, try various methods until you find one or more that you resonate with.

Meditation is a powerful way of connecting to Source, to your inner being, and to your spiritual support team. During meditation, clear your mind and set the intentions you wish to see enter into physical existence. Nurture the seeds by meditating on them whenever you feel moved to do so, visualizing yourself in the outcome you wish to see, and finding the feeling of it being manifested. Mysticism author Neville Goddard taught that to assume the feeling of the wish fulfilled attracts the physical manifestation of it. Goddard writes, "When you enter the state you desire to express and believe it is true, no earthly power can stop it from objectifying itself" (Goddard, 2012).

Because writing is a powerful way of bringing things into being, you can write out your intentions. Whether you write them out in a journal or for a spell (or both) is up to you. In addition to a manifestation journal, you can also keep a spell jar in which you keep all of your intentions and burn them when they manifest to release their energy into the universe.

Another way to seed your intentions is to fill a pouch with objects that represent them, and include a piece of paper with your written intentions, rolled into a scroll and tied round with ribbon in a color that is associated with your desire, such as red for love. You may wish to create a ritual around this, which can be as simple or as complicated as you like. You can keep the talisman in the corresponding gua of your home (see appendix C for the locations), and add to it on a regular basis to nurture the growth.

See appendix B for a full moon ritual to amplify the intentions you seed on the new moon.

Room for Growth

Whether you feel as though your life is at a standstill or there is something waiting in the wings for you, it can be helpful to better understand the current energies in your life, and how and where they are flowing. There may be more to a situation than is immediately evident; it could have the potential to take you further than you ever dreamed possible. Use this spread (see illustration 5-2) to gain clarity on growth that is already underway, how to shepherd it into its fullest potential, and where there are opportunities for expansion.

Suggested questions:

1. Where am I currently growing?
2. How can I nurture this?
3. How can I make it work for me?
4. How will I know when it has matured?
5. Where do I need to spread my wings?
6. What do I need to further develop?
7. What should I nurture?
8. Where should I focus my efforts at this time?

Illustration 5-2: Room for Growth

The Untrodden Path

There are times when we need to make our own way in life, to carve out a path of our own. This can have to do with making your way in the world, shifting your career path or perspective, changing directions, creating a new life for yourself, or starting a business. This spread (see illustration 5-3) is designed to help you look ahead with wisdom and clarity, to guide you through the shifts, and to otherwise prepare for what might lie before you.

Suggested questions:

1. Where do I need to forge my own path?
2. What underbrush do I need to clear?
3. What is the best way forward?
4. Where does this path lead?
5. Some hidden surprises along the way.
6. Some potential stumbling blocks I need to be aware of.
7. What can I do to prepare?
8. Advice from my inner being.

Illustration 5-3: The Untrodden Path

Stopping to Smell the Roses

When we become so duty-bound and busy that we hardly have a moment for ourselves, it is important to make the space and time to get back to what brings us joy and pleasure. Stopping to examine our schedules and routines and how they are and are not working for us is a necessity every now and then. This spread (see illustration 5-4) allows you to take a closer look at what needs adjustment in your life and where you would benefit from pausing to breathe in the sweetness life has to offer.

Suggested questions:

1. Where should I linger more?
2. What do I need to stop and examine?
3. What isn't working for me?
4. Where do I need to reassess my obligations?
5. What enjoyment am I missing?
6. How can I welcome in more joy?
7. In what ways should I be embracing life more?
8. What are the thorns I should avoid?
9. Where can I find life's sweetest nectar?

Illustration 5-4: Stopping to Smell the Roses

I Direct My Attention

If you've ever felt like you have too many irons in the fire and every day is a juggling act, it can be helpful to know where to start first. The most pressing thing to focus on isn't always readily apparent. Sometimes it is the thing you forgot about, the thing that slipped through the cracks, that is getting ready to ignite and cause an explosion. This is a spread (see illustration 5-5) for busy people everywhere.

Suggested questions:

1. What needs my focused attention right now?
2. What actions should I take?
3. How should I approach it?
4. Where does it need restructuring?
5. What are the best ways for me to carve out space for it?
6. How can I honor it?
7. How can I develop it to its greatest potential?

Illustration 5-5: I Direct My Attention

Spells & Rituals
Amplify Your Divine Radiance

Summon the beauty within and envision the best version of yourself. Best performed on a Sunday or Friday during the waxing or full moon.

What You Need:

The Emperor or the Empress card

Your significator card

Perfume or cologne

Scented candles

Your favorite jewelry

Your best outfit

A bouquet of your favorite flowers or evergreen sprigs

Dress in an outfit that makes you feel the most radiant. Put on your favorite jewelry, spritz on some fragrance, and arrange your hair and makeup (optional, of course) however you like. Set the mood with music that makes you feel relaxed and at ease, and light scented candles for ambiance. Your gift to yourself, an act of self-love, is a bouquet of flowers or evergreens. This is both a gift to yourself and an offering to your inner god or goddess. Place the Emperor or the Empress card, depending on your preference, over your significator card in front of the bouquet. Once you are in a relaxed and peaceful state, say the following three times:

> *I call to my inner God/Goddess, my divine inner being*
> *I honor you and send you my love*
> *As I honor my beauty from within*
> *I call upon my divine radiance*
> *And summon it to fill me and expand*
> *And amplify, increasing by the power of three*
> *Illuminating me as I glow with my unique divinity*
> *And I am filled and surrounded with well-being*
> *In body and mind, for now and all time.*

Meditate, visualizing yourself at your most radiant and beautiful, honoring the truest beauty that comes from within. See yourself as you wish to be and hold this in your mind, letting it imprint as your new self-image. Repeat this spell as often as you like until your new vision of yourself has firmly taken root in your mind and this is how you see yourself from now on. Your body is versatile and will comply with your self-image over time.

Corn Fertility Spell

This versatile spell can be used for fertility or financial abundance and is easily tailored to anything you want to manifest. Best performed on a Monday or Friday (for fertility) or Thursday (for financial abundance) during the new, waxing, or full moon.

What You Need:
A fertile patch of ground
Sweet corn seeds
Objects to bury that represent your desired manifestation, e.g., dolls if you are trying to
    conceive or coins for financial abundance

Corn has long been regarded by many cultures as representative of fertility, the sacred feminine, good luck, and abundance. The best time to plant corn depends partly on your region. Sweet corn grows best when planted in soil above 60°F (16°C); for super-sweet corn, it should be above 65°F (18°C). It is not recommended to start corn seeds indoors, as the roots don't hold up well to transplanting. Soak dry sweet corn seeds in room-temperature water overnight the night before planting. As you drop each one into the water, focus your intentions, visualizing your desires coming to fruition as the corn sprouts and matures, seeing this happening in your mind's eye.

Plant seeds four to six inches apart at a depth of one and a half to two inches. If you plant in rows, space them thirty to thirty-six inches apart. Bury your talismans of choice—whether this is coins for increased financial abundance, dolls if you are trying to conceive, or something else representing your desire—between the rows, and/ or between the seeds. How many of the objects you bury is up to you. Then, water the area well, including the places where you have buried the talismans, and visualize them growing too.

Visit the area often during the growth process, visualizing and feeling into the manifestation of your intention each time you are there. This is easy to do while you are pulling weeds, as you can envision the removal of obstacles to reaching your goal. Your corn is ready to harvest when the silk starts to turn brown; check the kernels and make sure they look full.

Before removing the corn from the stalk, give thanks to the earth, and thank the spirit of the corn. To harvest, twist and pull the ear downward, visualizing as you do so your intentions coming into full manifestation as you harvest the rich bounty of the seeds you have planted, bringing it into your life in its fully manifested form. Enjoy the corn cooked with a delicious meal and savor with gratitude what you have cocreated in all its sweetness, knowing that the successful outcome corresponds with the sure success of your manifestations. Leave the objects buried.

The Corn Husk Knot

Focus your intentions into a corn husk knot to manifest your desired outcome. Best performed on a Monday or Friday (for fertility) or Thursday (for abundance) during the new or waxing moon.

What You Need:
Nine corn husks of equal length
Length of twine
Any decorations, such as beads of a certain color, that you wish to work into the knots

Because corn traditionally symbolizes abundance, stability, fertility, good luck, and protection, this spell works especially well for those types of intentions. Knot magic is a way of focusing your intention on a particular outcome or change you wish to see.

Begin by getting clear on your intention. Then, as you focus on the outcome you want, such as an increase in income (choosing a specific amount is helpful), braid three corn husks together. Before knotting them at each end, visualize your desire manifesting into being and feel as fully as possible what it will feel like when the result arrives, then tie the knot. If you work with color correspondences and are focusing on financial abundance, for example, you can braid green and/or gold beads into the braids. Feel free to get creative about what you work into your braids, keeping in mind that the more closely the additions correspond to your intention, the more potency they will have.

Braid the other corn husks so that you end up with three braided strands. You can braid the three strands together and tie each end together with twine, or you can tie the three braids together at one end with the twine. You may choose to tie a loop at one end and hang your talisman somewhere of significance to you, such as in the wealth gua (see appendix C for its location) for money spells. You can also combine the braids in a more elaborate knot and use it as an altarpiece. After your outcome has manifested, safely burn the knot while giving thanks, then bury the ashes.

Finding What Is Lost

Use this all-purpose spell to find lost things. This spell can be performed anytime.

Begin by picturing the object you wish to find, holding it firmly in your mind's eye. See yourself walking up to the object and picking it up or, if it is heavy, placing your hand out and drawing it to you like a magnet. Visualize this as you repeat the following three times:

> *What is mine returns to me*
> *Only what is for my highest good*
> *What once was lost, now I see*
> *By the power of three, it comes to me*
> *My missing object now is found*
> *As this spell circles round*
> *So it is and blessed be.*

Sometimes, as you visualize yourself walking up to the object, you will see clues as to its location. It is also good to keep in mind that something may have left your life for a specific purpose, is unable to return to you, or is not meant for you at this time. This can be for karmic reasons, for your highest good or someone else's, or it may serve the purpose of teaching a lesson.

Chapter 6
June: The Strawberry Moon

As the berries of the field ripen into their fullness, the Strawberry Moon shines its light above them. June's full moon is also known as the Rose Moon, the Mead Moon, the Dyad Moon, or the Hot Moon.

The Strawberry Moon tarot spreads included in this chapter explore what is ripe and ready for the picking, where there is sweetness that is yet undiscovered, what new deliciousness can be created, how to find relief in sticky situations, and what would benefit from pruning.

The spells and rituals in this chapter include drawing in positive circumstances, amplifying the sweetness in life, and creating a good luck talisman.

Tuning in Before a Reading

Connecting with your higher self, or getting into alignment, before a reading helps to ensure the best and most accurate results. From an aligned state, you are better able to receive and understand the wisdom being offered to you through the cards, which are another way of connecting with divine intelligence. Nikola Tesla wisely said, "My brain is only a receiver. In the universe there is a core from which we obtain knowledge, strength, and inspiration" (Excellence Reporter, 2019). Many practitioners find it effective to call on their allies before beginning a reading to invite higher guidance to come through, allowing for a greater understanding of the messages that are meant to be conveyed.

Simply sitting with the intention of connecting to your inner wisdom is a great way to begin. You may feel a sense of calm and peace envelop you; this lets you know you're tuned in and in alignment. At this point, you can call on any guides, angels, and other high-vibrational allies and ask them to support you in the reading and bring to you the understanding that will most benefit you, or the knowledge and guidance that is for your highest good according to the questions that you ask. The wording is up to you. Once you make this a part of your practice, you will find that your readings become more meaningful when you have the full support of your allies close at hand.

Spreads

Tasting the Sweetness of the Vine

There is a saying that timing is everything. While it may not be everything, exactly, it can be helpful to know the best actions to take, as the choicest moment to advance to the next step is not always obvious. Use this spread (see illustration 6-1) as a guide to help you gain insight on what is available to you that may not be readily apparent; how the fruits of the vine, those opportune situations, factor into the various elements of your life; and how you can make the most of them.

Suggested questions:

1. What is becoming in my life?
2. What is ripe and ready for the picking?
3. How can I fully savor it?
4. What role does this ingredient play in my life?
5. How does it contribute to other areas of my life?
6. What can I learn from it?
7. How can I amplify the sweetness in my life?
8. What actions am I guided to take at this time?

Illustration 6-1: Tasting the Sweetness of the Vine

When Your Significator Card Changes

That we are always changing is no secret; even our cells are constantly being remade. Receiving upgrades, restructuring belief systems, and changing thought patterns are all ways we remake ourselves throughout our lives. As we learn and grow, these changes are inevitable. So it makes sense that the card you choose to represent you will also likely change as you do, as you place at the forefront different priorities, goals, and core beliefs.

Feeling as though your significator card no longer resonates with you may prompt you to make a new selection. You can do this by tuning in and asking the cards to reveal your new significator. If you receive more than one card, don't be surprised; these can represent different aspects of you. Especially if you shuffle overhand and allow the resonant cards to fall out of the deck, you may receive cards that reveal various parts of your personality, experience, mindset, or goals.

If you receive multiples, keep these in mind and allow your guidance to point you to which significator card makes sense for you to use in a particular reading. Often, it will be the card that most closely aligns with the energies of the reading or with your queries.

Hidden Treasures

We don't know what we can't see. There may be times when there is something so wonderful for us, if only we knew it was there. Whether you are looking for answers regarding relationships, career and financial opportunities, or untapped spiritual gifts, this spread (see illustration 6-2) can help you uncover hidden gems that are available to you. Sometimes you just have to know where to look.

Suggested questions:

1. What hidden opportunities are available to me?
2. Where can I find them?
3. What are my first steps?
4. How can I develop them?
5. How should I apply them in my life?
6. What are my next steps?
7. What should I do to prepare myself?
8. Where will this lead me?
9. What is the best and highest possible outcome?

Illustration 6-2: Hidden Treasures

Aligned Manifestation

While it is true that we create our own realities, when we line up with the current supporting energies—lunar or otherwise—they can assist our creations more fully and allow them to come into being quicker and in ways that are divinely aligned to our highest purpose and potential. Use this spread (see illustration 6-3) to shed light on what manifestations it would be most beneficial to put your energies into at this time for the outcome that is most favorable to you.

Suggested questions:

1. What are the current energies that can support my manifestations?
2. How can I best align with these energies?
3. What manifestations are especially supported at this time?
4. How should I approach these manifestations?
5. What actions can I take that will support me?
6. Where should I focus my efforts now?
7. How can I see this through to fruition?
8. Guidance from my higher self.
9. A message from my guides.
10. Wisdom from the universe.

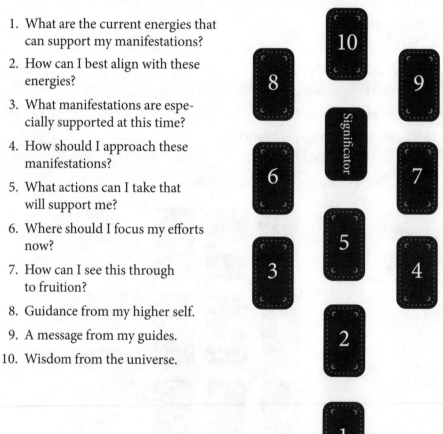

Illustration 6-3: Aligned Manifestation

Sweet Relief

Sometimes we find ourselves in situations that would well be called conundrums; we just can't see a way out, or any choice we make would be fraught with difficulty. Like brambles that catch at our ankles, we can feel trapped, stuck, as though whichever way we turn will result in pain and further discord. Tarot (see illustration 6-4) can help us to consider solutions we may not have considered, and it can also shine a light on painful truths. The beauty of divine guidance is that it never pulls any punches; you can always rely on the cards to tell it like it is and to provide solutions where we may not have seen them before.

Suggested questions:

1. What is my area of greatest need?
2. What factors are contributing to it?
3. What is the underlying source of the problem?
4. How can I find relief?
5. How can I support myself at this time?
6. What support is already around me that I should employ?
7. What is the best action I can take now?
8. What can I do to bring full about a full resolution?

Illustration 6-4: Sweet Relief

Pruning the Branches

When it comes to landscaping, trimming back branches is essential for the health and growth of a tree, as it can prevent issues later on and encourage future vitality by removing portions that are dead and dying, succumbing to disease, and so on. It is sometimes the same with us; we may have a job that does not serve us or relationships that would be better for us to move away from or implement stronger boundaries around. There are many scenarios to which this could apply, but if you feel like there are parts of your life that aren't working for you, this spread (see illustration 6-5) can help you gain clarity on how best to proceed.

Suggested questions:

1. Where do I need greater clarity?
2. What is ready to leave my life?
3. What habits or routines do I need to reassess?
4. Where am I bogged down?
5. What actions would it benefit me to take?
6. What insight is there for me?
7. What relationships aren't serving me?
8. What is my best course of action regarding those relationships?
9. How can I make my life more fruitful?

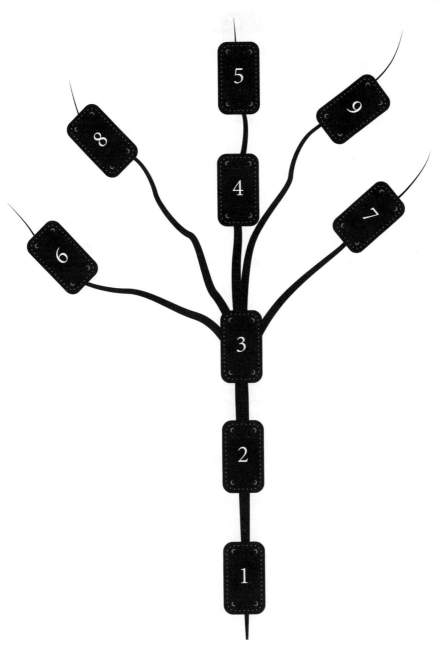

Illustration 6-5: Pruning the Branches

Spells & Rituals
Positivity Magnet

Create a vision board to manifest your desires. Best if started on a Sunday, Tuesday, or Wednesday during a new or waxing moon.

What You Need:
Poster board
Old magazines
Glue
Scissors

When it comes to attracting what we want, how we feel is everything. What we fill our minds with in turn fills our energy and our vibration, drawing to us more of the same. Bringing more positivity into your life is accomplished by feeling positive. Writer and teacher Elena Sonnino recommends choosing a word to embody. She writes, "You may find that words choose you rather than the other way around. It isn't so much the word that matters—but how you allow yourself to interact with the feeling behind the word" (Sonnino, 2018).

Creating a vision board is a powerful way to support your embodiment of a word. For this vision board, first choose a word that resonates with you (or let it choose you). Once you have your word—whether it is positivity, joy, happiness, or another word of your choosing—sit with it for a while and visualize all the things you associate with it. These can be people, places, pets, or situations that help you to feel what the word embodies. You can also visualize yourself in situations not yet manifested that you associate with the feeling of that word. As you do this, let all the best aspects of the visualization fill your emotional well until you are really feeling your word and everything it represents to the fullest possible capacity.

Once you have set your intention for what you wish to embody by feeling your word and bringing it into your vibration, it's time to create your vision board. Have fun doing this; you can even involve a friend or family member, and support your endeavor by making a playlist of music that makes you feel uplifted, vibrant, happy, and any other feelings you associate with your word. Listen to this music while you create your vision board. Gather up old magazines and create a collage on a piece of poster board or cardboard with your word at the top. Every time you look at it, it will remind you of your word and serve as a visual representation of all the things you hope to be or to manifest as a result of this work, and any changes you wish for it to bring about.

Making a commitment to feeling into your word daily, even if only for several minutes, will yield rewards over time, as your efforts are compounded every time you practice it. Because we attract what we feel, the more you allow yourself to feel your word, the more changes you will start to see as a result. You can use this process to rewire your thinking; every time you catch yourself in a negative thought or emotion, bring your word to mind and let it shift your focus into more positive thoughts. Be gentle with yourself throughout this process; changing your mindset is no small task, and you are to be commended for applying the effort, for showing up for yourself, and for being your own best advocate.

Sweetness Amplified

Amplify your intentions to the universe with a crystal grid. Best performed on a Sunday or Thursday during a full moon.

What You Need:
A sacred geometry grid of your choosing
Crystals, cleansed and purified (see page 45)
Sage (optional)
Wand or athame (optional)
One white candle

Bringing sacred geometry into your magical practice is a powerful way to amplify your intentions. We can observe the patterns of sacred geometry, such as spirals, in the cosmos and in so many things all around us, most noticeably in nature, architecture, and music. These universal patterns are recognized by many as the building blocks of reality as we know it, the mathematically informed shapes that give matter form and substance.

You may already have a preferred pattern but if not, the Flower of Life or the Seed of Life are both good choices for this amplification grid. You can purchase crystal grids from metaphysical shops or find one online to print out. If you use a printed copy, you can color it in if you like and focus on your intentions as you do so, infusing it with the energy.

When choosing your crystals for the grid, keep in mind that the lines help to flow the energy, and the points where the grid lines intersect are like points of interest that map the energy. The crystals will be working in tandem with one another, so choose crystals that are relevant to your intention. The center crystal is the focus stone, or focal point, to which you send your intentions, and it amplifies this to the surrounding crystals. The crystals surrounding the focus stone are the way stones, which enhance the energy of the intentions with their own unique energies. On the outer circle are the desire stones, which add supporting energy for fine-tuning the manifestation. Add quartz points along the grid lines to further amplify and direct the flow of energy; these should be pointing outward, away from the focus stone to send the energy out into the universe to be manifested.

Before setting up the grid, consecrate yourself, the area, and the tools you will be using with sage, intention, or by any other means you prefer. Ground (see appendix A for a full grounding meditation), cast a sacred circle (see appendix B), call in high-vibrational allies, and ask for divine protection and guidance. State your intention, either aloud or silently, and thank the crystals you will be working with, asking them to contribute their energies to the grid for your purpose.

Place the focus stone in the center, concentrating on your intention as you do so. Focus on this as you place the crystals on the grid, keeping in mind the energies of each crystal and what it can contribute. As you place the crystals, work outward clockwise from the center, visualizing the energy around your desire manifesting and growing with each placement.

After the grid is complete, activate it either with your wand or by intention, calling in divine white light and sending it to the focus stone. Visualize the light emanating out from the center and activating all the crystals on the grid, connecting them all, as it expands and fully surrounds the grid and then envelops you completely. Focus your intentions toward the grid, then send them out to the universe as you visualize them expanding from the center and outward.

As you light the candle, infuse it with the intention to amplify the grid and surround and infuse it with the white light of high-vibrational divine love and sacred protection. Give thanks to the divine, to your allies, and to the crystals. You may wish to meditate and visualize your intentions coming to life before grounding and closing the circle. Let the candle burn down completely. The energies of your grid will be the strongest during the first three days after activation, and it will hold the energy of your intentions as long the grid remains intact.

A Good Luck Talisman

Create a good luck charm that you can take with you anywhere. Best performed on a Wednesday during a waxing moon.

What You Need:
Your significator card
Frankincense (resin or incense)
One green candle
One gold candle
A lucky charm
Three gold coins or Chinese feng shui coins

Good luck has more to do with your beliefs than anything else. If you believe you are lucky, you will be; if you believe good things are coming to you, they are. Of course, the inverse is also true, so keeping your intentions aligned with the outcome you wish to have gives a powerful boost to this talisman. If you believe that when you wear it or carry it with you good things will come to you, then the universe will prove you right.

The charm you choose can be a pendant that you wear around your neck, part of a charm bracelet, or something that you keep on your altar or workspace, in your pocket or wallet, or that you place in the wealth gua of your living space (see appendix C). To begin, purify and consecrate the objects you will be using for this spell. Place your significator card face-up in front of the candles, and have the frankincense nearby. If you are using Chinese coins and they are not tied together, arrange them in a triangle shape around the card, with one coin at the top center of the card and the other two on either side of its base. If your coins are tied together, place them on top of the card; you will use them again in a moment. Cast a circle (see appendix B) and call in high-vibrational allies if you wish.

Light the frankincense and pass your lucky talisman through the smoke as you chant three times:

Three times three
Good luck comes to me
Sacred and blessed may this talisman be
Expanding good fortune

And drawing it to me
Lucky me, lucky me, lucky me
So it is and blessed be.

Light the green candle and move the talisman clockwise around it as you chant the above. Light the gold candle and repeat the process. If you are using Chinese coins that are tied together, hold them by the top of the string in one hand as you hold the talisman in your other hand, then circle the coins clockwise around the charm while repeating the incantation another three times. Place the talisman on your significator card as the candles burn down. If you used coins tied together, place them on your talisman.

You may choose to meditate on any specific intentions as the candles burn down, or if your intention is overall good luck, let the candles burn down completely, and be sure to let them go out on their own (never blow them out). When the candles are out, your talisman is ready, and you can ground your energy (see appendix A for a full grounding meditation) and close the circle. You may wish to reenergize it by repeating this process every full moon.

Chapter 7
July: The Buck Moon

In the month of July, we can witness new antlers sprouting from the heads of bucks running wild through the forest, lending this month's moon its name, the Buck Moon. July's moon is also referred to as the Thunder Moon, the Hay Moon, or the Wort Moon.

The Buck Moon tarot spreads included in this chapter examine what is developing, how to embrace what is emerging, nurturing new situations and developments, gaining control over unruly situations, and where you need to let go.

The spells and rituals in this chapter include awakening gifts and talents, reining in chaotic energies and situations to harness them into something ordered and stable, an energy healing ritual, and a thistle protection spell.

Spreads
What Is Developing

Life is never still; even the very cells of our bodies are constantly vibrating and meta-morphosing. Something is always developing, growing, changing, and becoming for us. If we are conscious creators of our own reality, we will often know what that is, but even so, the universe always seems to have something more underway, some surprise in store, even if it is in the way things come to you. Use this spread (see illustration 7-1) to take a peek into what is unfolding for you that you would benefit from being aware of and gaining insight into.

Suggested questions:

1. What is currently developing in my life?
2. How will it impact me?
3. What energies are supporting it?
4. How can I direct my energy to support it?
5. What can I do to nurture its development?
6. How can I help bring it to its greatest potential?
7. What does its optimal manifestation look like?
8. Where will this take me?

Illustration 7-1: What Is Developing

Preparing to Receive

Being aware of what is headed toward us allows us to be better prepared. This spread (see illustration 7-2) can help you gain insight on opportunities, relationships, or anything else that might be on its way to you so you can be ready to receive or reroute, as the case may be. Preparing energetically is one of the most important ways you can enter a state of readiness, whether that is to brace for impact, redirect your thinking, or to welcome something with an open heart and mind.

Suggested questions:

1. What is ready to enter my life now?
2. What can I contribute to ensure its successful emergence?
3. How can I best receive it?
4. What is the greatest possible impact it can have on me?
5. How can I use it to my highest potential?
6. What impact beyond me can this have?
7. Advice for me energetically during this time.
8. A message from my higher self.

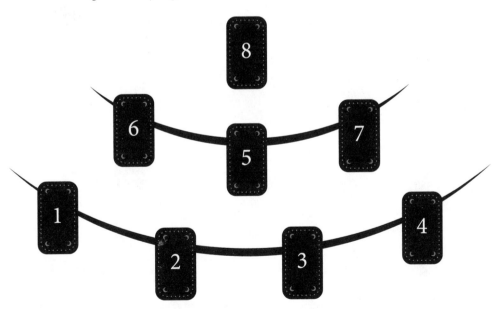

Illustration 7-2: Preparing to Receive

Nurturing Your Seedlings

Preparing for new growth is like sprinkling energetic fertilizer on the soil of your manifestations. When we add nutrients, water, and otherwise care for the new life in a garden, we ensure that it will thrive and bring joy for a long time to come. This spread (see illustration 7-3) can help you recognize new positive aspects and situations entering your life, how to nurture them for the greatest possible outcome, and what to do to ensure they will bear fruit later on.

Suggested questions:

1. What new growth is entering my life?

2. How can I prepare for it?

3. What should I clear out or release to ensure its greatest potential?

4. How will the new growth help me?

5. How will it impact me spiritually?

6. How will it impact me emotionally?

7. Where is it leading me?

8. What will this ultimately become?

9. What fruits will it bear?

Illustration 7-3: Nurturing Your Seedlings

Taming the Wild Overgrowth

Like an invasive plant that enters a garden and takes over, sometimes situations can spin out of control as they gather momentum in a certain direction and seem to take over every aspect of your life. When things feel like they're slipping out of your grasp, use this spread (see illustration 7-4) to help you gain insight on how to approach the situation and how to resolve it for your highest good, as sometimes a full uprooting is needed, while other times it may be better to simply trim back the overgrowth.

Suggested questions:

1. What in my life needs reigning in?
2. How can I best approach it?
3. What is the best step I can take now?
4. What is the ideal resolution?
5. How can I achieve this?
6. What changes will this bring about?
7. How does this situation fit into the bigger picture?

Illustration 7-4: Taming the Wild Overgrowth

Letting Go

It can be difficult to release something when you don't know what the outcome will be. Sometimes you feel as though if you just think about it long enough, you'll be able to improve it in some way. But when you're feeling resistance about something you want, it can't come to you. Whether you're unintentionally stifling something from manifesting by subconsciously keeping a white-knuckle grip on it or you're having trouble releasing something from the past and find it hard to move on, this spread (see illustration 7-5) can help you to take an honest look at what you need to let go of and how doing so will benefit you.

Suggested questions:

1. Where do I need to loosen my grip?
2. What do I need to let go of?
3. How can I let go?
4. How will letting go benefit me?
5. Where do I need to surrender?
6. Where do I need to shift my beliefs?
7. How will this impact me?
8. How can I better trust the universe?
9. How should I move forward?

Illustration 7-5: Letting Go

On the Timing of Spells and Rituals

If you want to perform a certain ritual or spell but the current planetary energies or day of the week do not support it, begin your ritual by stating, *I neutralize all energies, planetary and otherwise, that would interfere with the successful outcome of this magical working.* It is generally optimal to work with the energies that will support the outcomes you desire, as it gives your work an added boost, but if you are having a magical emergency, you can call on the support of high-vibrational allies and proceed anyway, leading with the above statement.

You Get What You See

The objects in your environment—everything from the colors you choose for your furnishings to what you hang on your wall—all carry a vibration that affects your mood and your reality. Over time, you may notice that the things you see on a regular basis begin to manifest in some way. If you want to take a trip to Iceland, hang a photo of Iceland on your wall; of course, this will not instantly manifest the trip for you, but it will support it energetically by creating a vibrational momentum that builds every time you give your attention to the subject. Bringing flowers into your space can translate into more flowers or beauty. You may notice that you started with one sea-foam-green piece of decor, and it has blossomed into many because, well, like attracts like. This is the key principle behind what makes vision boards so effective.

Tarot cards are wonderfully symbolic objects to display. If you want to usher in emotional renewal, display the Six of Cups or the Ace of Cups. If you want to bring a new opportunity into your life, keep the Ace of Wands in a place where you will see it often. This symbolism, a type of sympathetic magic that is based on the law of attraction, is one reason tarot cards are used in spells. Your significator card is one way for you to create desired change in your life. Displaying your card next to a card that represents something you are looking to call to you is a way of visually aligning yourself with its energy.

Gathering Momentum

According to Abraham-Hicks, it takes the law of attraction sixteen to seventeen seconds for a thought to gather momentum and begin to manifest vibrationally. Keeping this time frame in mind when you are meditating or saying mantras and affirmations can be helpful. In this way you create, and plant, seeds of desire, and sitting with the thought of something you want to manifest for at least that amount of time begins the creation process.

Supporting this with emotions, feeling as though the desired result has already come about, lends powerful support to your intentions. Continuing on the same train of thought is like a snowball rolling downhill—the longer it rolls, the more snow it gathers and the bigger it gets. Every time you focus on something, you add to its momentum, whether it is something you want or not. Your higher self is constantly focused on what you want, and this adds further to the momentum.

Weaving this practice into your rituals and meditations can boost outcomes dramatically. A fun experiment is to try doing this on a daily basis and see how long it takes you to manifest a specific thing or outcome. Try starting with something small that you believe you can easily have, remembering that you have to be in the space of allowing, a place of no resistance, to receive it.

Spells & Rituals

Awakening Your Spiritual Gifts: A Tea Ritual

Activate your clairgifts with this potent tea ritual. Best begun on a Monday or Wednesday during a dark, new, or full moon. *Do not drink this tea if you are pregnant.*

What You Need:

One bag of yarrow tea

One bag of jasmine tea

One bag of mugwort tea

As we each have a propensity for different spiritual gifts, the results of this spell will vary for everyone. It is important to keep in mind that the purpose of this magical working is to send your intention of awakening a gift or gifts out to the universe. Know that this request will be answered; however, there may be work for you to do, such as healing or gaining awareness and clarity in certain areas of your life, before something is ready to be activated. There are cases where spiritual gifts are instantly awakened, but those usually follow a severe trauma of some kind.

It is also good to be aware that, after doing this, you may be guided on a healing journey or feel drawn to certain crystals, books, or teachers—all of this is guidance that is in answer to your asking. Pay keen attention to the ideas and intuition that come to you, as these can be valuable nuggets of guidance from the universe. Following these trails can lead to some of the most interesting and rewarding explorations that pay off in unexpected ways.

Before beginning this ritual, ground (see appendix A for a full grounding meditation) and come into alignment. Gather your tea bags and use your intention to surround and fill each one with high-vibrational love and light. Ask for divine protection and support, then send gratitude to the herbs for their support. This is a powerful herbal collaboration, so this ritual should be approached with reverence.

Yarrow brings clarity and protection, and awakens psychic abilities. Jasmine, which is linked with lunar energy, encourages divinatory abilities and prophetic dreams. Mugwort awakens psychic abilities and lends itself to lucid dreaming and a deeper spiritual connection.

If the tea bags have strings attached, braid the three together to symbolically and energetically unite the triad. Fill a teacup with hot water and hold them above the water, spinning them clockwise over the cup while repeating the following incantation three times. If you are using loose-leaf tea, place equal amounts of each tea together in a single infuser, which you can then gently spin clockwise above the water while repeating three times:

> *By the power of the moon*
> *I open my eyes*
> *To see beyond the veil*
> *To see the unseen*
> *To access worlds within and without*
> *My senses awaken*
> *My chakras align*
> *I receive knowledge*
> *And wisdom divine*
> *My spiritual gifts now awaken.*

Let the tea steep for several minutes, then drink it in a meditative state while focusing on the intention of awakening your clairgifts. Keep in mind that your vibration determines the energies you connect with; if you are in a high-vibrational state, you will be aligned with high-vibrational energies.

Turning Chaos into Order

Stabilize a chaotic situation and transform it according to the highest possible outcome. Best started on a Wednesday or Saturday during a waxing moon.

What You Need:
A variety of items representing the chaotic situation you are experiencing, such as photos and physical objects
Black tourmaline, cleansed and charged (see page 45)
Tiger's eye, cleansed and charged (see page 45)
Your significator card

This ritual is ideal if you are experiencing something chaotic in your life that needs reigning in; it works for any situation or circumstance that you want to transform so it is more organized and stable.

First, cleanse the items you have gathered with the method of your choosing; set these up in a random order on your altar or workspace to symbolize their current state. Because you will be leaving them there until the situation changes, it is best if you put them in a place that you will see often, that you will not need to use for anything else, and that will remain undisturbed by children or pets; you should avoid moving them for as long as they are there, which will be until the situation stabilizes in the manner you will set forth here.

Place the cleansed and charged crystals on your significator card, symbolizing the infusion of grounding and clarity that is taking place for you during this ritual. Cast a circle if you wish (see appendix B) and call in high-vibrational allies, asking for their assistance with the stabilization of the matter at hand.

Turn your attention to the items you have chosen to symbolize your current situation. These may include photographs of the person or people involved, images cut out from magazines that represent the various components, and objects such as house keys that are directly connected to the situation. Arrange the items symbolically in a way that represents how you would like things to be. For instance, you may want to organize them in rows, or place them on or next to one another in a way that signifies the projected outcome (a house key could go on top of a picture of a person, which could be placed on a photo of a house, and so on). Once this is done, say three times while focusing on the new outcome you are envisioning:

What was not working
Now is fixed
Where chaos was
Now structure reigns
Order and stability
Balance and solidity
Brings forth happy outcomes
For the highest good of all
All is stable
All is well
So it is
And blessed be.

You can add specific wording to the above incantation that reflects how you want to see the circumstances change. When you are ready, you can ground your energy (see appendix A for a full grounding meditation) and close the circle. Leave the layout where it is until the situation has changed as you envisioned it. When you receive the desired results, give thanks to your allies.

Light of Positivity: A Healing Ritual

Use this ritual to send healing to a person or situation. Best started on a Thursday during a new or waxing moon.

What You Need:

One white candle

This simple meditation can be very powerful, especially as you come back to it and feed its energy, allowing it to gather momentum until it manifests the desired results. Cleanse the candle with saltwater, ground and center (see appendix A for a full grounding meditation), then cast a circle if you wish (see appendix B) and call in high-vibrational allies. If you are sending healing to others, ask the higher self or selves of all involved for permission to do so before beginning. If you have their consent, you may proceed knowing that this ritual is divinely supported; do not proceed if you hear or sense a *no*. There may be reasons beyond your understanding for a negative response; it could be that the person is experiencing something that they need to proceed through as part of their soul's journey.

To begin, light the candle as you focus on your intention, picturing the situation you wish to infuse with positive energy and directing the light of the flame to the situation. Say:

I send healing light to this situation
I send love, peace, and guidance to all involved
The light of this flame heals all wounds
Heals all circumstances and every person
To the highest extent that they will allow
All according to their highest good
Let all be surrounded with high-vibrational divine light and love.

You may wish to replace the words "this situation" above with something more specific or any description of your choosing. Try to keep your wording clear, direct, and simple.

Sit before the candle flame and tune in, letting your eyelids droop to half-mast so that you are softly gazing at the flame. Envision the light expanding to surround the situation and all involved. Picture everyone that is part of it as clearly as possible, then visualize the light powerfully creating the best and highest outcome, whether that is healing or some other resolution. Send love and light to everyone who is part of it, requesting the support of high-vibrational allies, guides, and angels as you do so to maximize the impact.

Meditate for as long as you feel you need to, and let the candle burn down and extinguish on its own. Be sure to thank any allies and the higher selves of the person or people you are working with before closing. When you are ready, you can ground your energy and close the circle. Returning to this visualization on a regular basis—whether in ritual or in thought as you go about your day-to-day life—will continue to add power and energy to the healing.

A Thistle Protection Spell

Activate a thistle flower as a powerful talisman of protection. Best started on a Tuesday or Saturday during a dark or full moon.

What You Need:
Thistle flower
Your significator card
One black candle
Dragon's blood incense

This spell works best with thistle that you have found and picked in the wild (let the flower choose you), but if you did not come by your thistle in this way, sit with it in meditation before beginning your ritual and connect with it, send it gratitude, and ask for its assistance in protecting you. Use saltwater to cleanse the elements you will be working with; it is best to cleanse the flower simply with intention, envisioning white light surrounding it.

Ground and center (see appendix A for a full grounding meditation), cast a circle (see appendix B), and call in your high-vibrational allies. Place your significator card in the middle of your workspace and light the black candle as you focus your intention toward the flame. After the candle is infused with energies of protection, it is time to activate the protective properties of the thistle. Light the dragon's blood incense and circle it clockwise around the thistle flower while saying:

I remain protected for all time
In body, mind, spirit, and in every way

On every plane, across all times, dimensions, space, and realities
I am protected at all times
For now and always
I am protected at all times
From all harmful and unwanted energies, entities, and interference
On every level
This flower protects me now and always
This thistle keeps me safe
I empower this magical plant to protect me
It is a powerful talisman that ensures my protection
I am protected at all times.

Repeat the above incantation three times, circling the incense around the flower clockwise all the while. If you have the ability to see energy, you may be able to see the center of the thistle swirling like a magical vortex as you do this. This means that you have activated the protective powers of the plant and infused it with your magic.

Turn your attention to the candle and say:

As this candle burns, all harmful and negative energies around me
Melt away and dissolve, releasing into the earth to be neutralized
And the energy around me is transformed into a protective layer
A sphere of protection surrounds me always
It lets in only love and peace and high-vibrational light
Only high-vibrational energies may enter
Only high-vibrational energies may be
So it is and blessed be.

Let the candle burn down on its own, leaving your significator card where it is until the candle is out. When you are ready, ground your energy and close the circle. You can keep the thistle on your altar, if you have one, or in any other place that is significant to you. You may want to refresh the talisman every now and then by repeating this spell or simply choose a new thistle flower to perform this ritual once a year at a time that is significant to you.

Chapter 8
AUGUST: THE STURGEON MOON

Named for the fish that swim in abundance this time of year, the Sturgeon Moon shines during a time of plenty and is also known as the Dispute Moon, the Fruit Moon, or the Green Corn Moon.

The Sturgeon Moon tarot spreads included in this chapter guide you in connecting to abundance, tapping into gratitude, expanding your reach and influence, bringing more happiness and fun into your life, and gaining clarity on any unfinished business that could be blocking you and your manifestations.

The spells and rituals in this chapter include revealing upcoming opportunities, opening yourself to receive, and a money-drawing spell.

Cleansing Your Tarot Deck

Just as you energetically cleanse your crystals and any other magical tools you work with, it is also important to periodically cleanse your tarot cards. You should do this when you first purchase them, after others have handled the cards, following a reading you have given someone else, or any time you feel it is necessary. Keeping a piece of selenite on them whenever they are not in use ensures they are always clear of unwanted and stagnant energies.

You can also smudge them with sage, cedar, or ethically sourced palo santo, or spread them out on a cloth and let them sit in sunlight for about twenty minutes, ensuring that the light reaches every card. Professional tarot reader and author Brigit Esselmont recommends tuning in to universal energy and allowing it to flow through you and into the deck as you visualize it surrounded with protective white light. In this way, you establish or reestablish a bridge between you and the cards, connecting your energy with them in a powerful way.

Spreads

Connecting to Abundance

Abundance is all around us. Whether it is in the form of financial prosperity, or intangibles like love and happiness, we can all connect to an infinite supply that is available just for us. This spread (see illustration 8-1) is useful if you have been working on manifesting something and it hasn't materialized yet. It can also help to shed light on what is currently available to you and how you can let it in.

Suggested questions:

1. What abundance is currently available to me vibrationally?
2. In what ways am I blocking it?
3. How can I release the blocks?
4. Where do I need to shift my beliefs so that I can receive?
5. What else will help me to receive the abundance?
6. How can I receive this manifestation fully?
7. What further opportunities will this open up?
8. A message from my higher self.

Illustration 8-1: Connecting to Abundance

The Tarot Journal

Keeping a journal in which you record your spreads and interpretations can prove valuable over time. It is an ideal way to explore the meanings and how they apply to your life, both when you are new to the practice and as you become more experienced. You may find that your initial insights on certain cards shift over time as you flow through changes and as you become more intimately familiar with the nuances and symbolic meanings the cards may hold. If you work with different decks, you will find that each one offers its own unique wisdom, with varying levels of depth. Different decks have different personalities.

The journal is not only a record of your journey with tarot itself, but also of your personal connection with divine guidance. Because tarot is a tool that allows us to receive messages and information from the higher self, guides, angels, and other allies, a written record can yield valuable insights when reviewed months or even years later, allowing you to look in retrospect at the way events unfolded. When compared with your past interpretation of future events, it can be enlightening to analyze the way things actually happened versus what you predicted.

The journal can also be a useful teaching tool as you observe the events over a period of time and the cards that were revealed as indicators. Were there deeper meanings you didn't see during the initial reading that became evident later? Do your notes shed new light that is only apparent now? Did things happen that shifted the outcome of cards that predicted other possibilities at the time? As you're looking back on these earlier inscriptions, you may discover interesting patterns that can help you piece together certain bits of information and nuggets of wisdom that offer invaluable guidance.

The Horn of Plenty

Turning our attention to what we already have and really feeling appreciation for it helps to draw in more of it by activating it in our vibration. This spread (see illustration 8-2) helps you to see where you are already abundant and where it would be beneficial for you to focus to help draw in more of what you are seeking to manifest. Because your higher self knows exactly what it is you desire and what you want to bring about in your life, working with that guidance by calling on your inner wisdom before drawing the cards for this spread can help you to tap into the knowledge that will guide you closer to the realization of your dreams—a good practice to follow before every reading.

Suggested questions:

1. Where am I already abundant?
2. What can I focus on that will help me reach my goals?
3. What should I stop focusing on?
4. What is my next step forward?
5. Where will this lead me?
6. What is on its way to me now?
7. Guidance from my higher self.
8. A message from the universe.

Illustration 8-2: The Horn of Plenty

Expanding Your Reach

For business owners, creatives, and anyone seeking to make their mark in the world in some way, expanding the sphere of influence can be one of the most crucial parts of growing a business, increasing a client base, obtaining recognition, getting buyers for artwork, and so on. Use this spread (see illustration 8-3) to delve into ways you can effectively magnify your influence and gain prominence in your area of expertise.

Suggested questions:

1. How can I make more of an impact?
2. How can I expand my reach?
3. What talents, gifts, and abilities can I use to help me expand?
4. How can I apply these constructively?
5. In what ways do I need to reach beyond myself?
6. How can this help others?
7. What can I offer that is of the highest value?
8. Where do I need to grow to make the greatest impact?

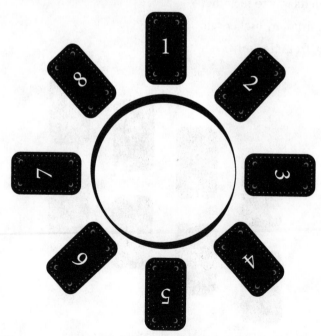

Illustration 8-3: Expanding Your Reach

Cause for Celebration

Nothing dissolves stuck and stagnant energies like excitement, happiness, and fun. These high-vibrational energies clear the way for abundance and manifestations to flow into your life with ease. This spread (see illustration 8-4) offers a check-in with the universe, and with your higher self, to bring you guidance on how you can open up to these energies and reveal what is waiting for you on the other side of that joy.

Suggested questions:

1. Where do I need more fun in my life?
2. How can I open up to joy?
3. How can I let in more excitement?
4. What will this new energy bring me?
5. What happy events are on their way to me now?
6. Guidance from my inner being.

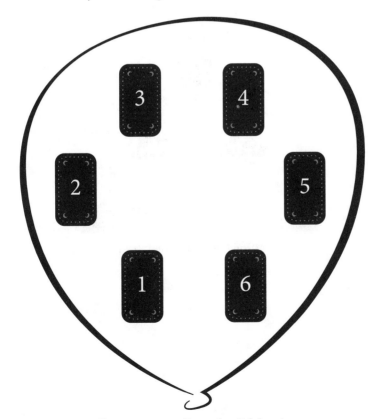

Illustration 8-4: Cause for Celebration

Unfinished Business

When we have unfinished business in our lives, it can cause an energy drain and create blocks to our success, sidetracking things that should be flowing to us. Sometimes, we are not even aware that we have loose ends that need to be taken care of. This spread (see illustration 8-5) can help to reveal any areas of your life where things need to be addressed so that you can move forward in prosperity and allow in all the abundance that is available to you.

Suggested questions:

1. Where are loose ends creating blocks for me?
2. Where is unfinished business creating an energy drain?
3. What do I need to do to wrap things up?
4. In what ways will this help me?
5. How will this help me on an energetic level?

Illustration 8-5: Unfinished Business

The Wisdom of Flowers

You may have heard flowers and herbs referred to as *plant allies*. Like crystals, and indeed every other form of naturally occurring matter that exists on the planet, plants are expressions of the earth's energy. Because different types of energy vibrate on different wavelengths, the expressions of those energies, like chamomile or yarrow, for example, carry different properties. When we are in need of that vibration, we can look to the ally that offers it.

Chamomile, especially in the form of tea, is calming and opens us to receive wisdom by helping us to enter a relaxed state. You may find that the fragrance of a rose lifts your spirits and elevates your vibration. Maybe a sudden craving for peppermint strikes you; you can trust that there is a reason, that your body carries its own wisdom and knows what will serve it best.

Including herbs, flowers, and other plants in your rituals can lend powerful vibratory qualities that enhance your intentions and your outcomes. If you feel drawn to a particular plant, trust your instincts; investigation of its properties may yield interesting results. It is likely that your inner guidance is signaling that it would benefit you in some way, whether by creating a ritual around it, adding it to your altar or workspace, or drinking it in a tea.

Reading Patterns

Sacred geometry provides the framework of the universe and informs our reality, giving shape to matter. The mathematical constants that provide the structure of geometrical shapes give rise to archetypal patterns that can be found in everything in existence, from atoms to galaxies. We see the same patterns produced throughout our reality: the spiral of a seashell is repeated in the spiral of a pinecone, a hurricane, and a galaxy, as micro moves to macro with perfect symmetry and ease. That all is one and we are all connected reveals itself again and again, not only in patterns but also in the knowing that we are made of the same materials as the stars. Astronomer Carl Sagan said, "The cosmos is all that is, or ever was, or ever will be. […] The cosmos is also within us. We're made of star stuff. We are a way for the cosmos to know itself" (Sagan, 1980).

To know truth, we have only to look within. But its evidence is also around us, in the patterns of nature, in the shapes of fallen leaves as form reveals itself and catches the eye. *Look here*, the universe seems to be saying, *I have a message for you*. It is thought that the Druids looked to the patterns of leaves in the trees to reveal what they would. Any natural form can offer clues as to what may come and to wisdom that will guide you. Look closer and notice what you see. The way twigs overlap may form a letter that holds meaning for you; the leaves in your favorite oak may part momentarily by the wind to form the shape of a heart. As Abraham-Hicks reminds us, "Pay attention to what's going on around you. Source is using every conceivable possible messenger to confirm and accentuate things that are important to you" (Hicks, 2004).

Spells & Rituals
Revealing Opportunities

Read tea leaves to divine the future. This ritual can be performed at any time.

What You Need:
Loose-leaf tea
Teacup and saucer

Tasseomancy, tassomancy, or *tasseography* is a form of divination using tea leaves to examine patterns that foretell future events. This can also be done with wine sediment or coffee grounds. Simply pour boiling water over a pinch of tea leaves; loose-leaf tea yields better results than using tea from a bag, which can be too fine. Let it steep for three to five minutes. While it is steeping, enter a meditative state and focus on the intention that you will receive important wisdom from the tea leaves that will be of use to you. If you have a specific question, concentrate on it during this time. Because this ritual is specifically about revealing opportunities, you can set your intention to see the opportunities that are forthcoming for you or tailor it according to your particular query.

Drink the tea, allowing a small bit of liquid to remain in the cup, along with the tea leaves at the bottom. If you are reading for yourself, hold the cup by the handle in your left hand and swirl the liquid and sediment around three times clockwise, focusing on your intention and question, if you have a specific one in mind (it is okay to leave it general and simply set the intention to receive any information that will benefit you). Turn the cup upside down and set it on the saucer so that all the liquid is released. Leave it there a moment to allow all of the liquid to drain out. If you are doing this reading for someone else, let them perform the previous steps. The reader will provide the interpretation for the sitter, or the person the reading is for.

The sitter is represented by the handle of the cup, which also indicates their residence. The bottom of the cup is the distant future, the side tells of events to come in the near future, and the rim indicates the present. The closer the leaves are to the handle, the sooner they are to being realized. The patterns and shapes indicated by the leaves will indicate symbols that can be observed as you turn the cup and look at it from various angles. As you examine it, forms and figures will emerge and become clearer in what they represent as well as in their relation to one another.

In the interpretation, your intuition will figure strongly. As you become familiar with the symbols and practice reading the patterns, you will develop connections to certain letters and symbols that will take on specific meanings for you. For example, a heart can indicate that love is about to enter your life or it can speak of your current relationship; the symbols around it can provide further meaning. It can also mean opening your heart on a spiritual level. Other symbols, such as anchors and triangles, are widely interpreted as indicators of good fortune, while birds can indicate news and messages.

The size of the objects should also be taken into consideration, as they indicate magnitude or importance. A very large anchor, for example, could foretell a sizable windfall. Lines indicate journeys, and their direction can show you where you are headed. The longer the line, the longer the journey. As the handle represents the home, where the line is in relation to it can provide clues as to the nature of the journey; a move to a new home could be depicted by a line that doesn't reach the handle, and a line arcing away from the handle and then back toward it could indicate a round-trip journey. Dots around symbols can indicate money. Leaves that adhere to the rim of the cup indicate an event depicted in the cup is soon to manifest.

When you begin your journey of interpretation, you may want to look up symbols to glean their commonly held meanings, but ultimately, you should trust your intuition to guide you. Much like tarot, the symbols will vary depending on your particular experience and outlook.

Opening Yourself to Receive

Clear blocks to abundance so you can receive to the fullest all that is in alignment with your highest good. Best begun on a Monday during a waxing or full moon.

What You Need:
One white candle
Your significator card
Frankincense (resin or incense)

Your intention is always of the utmost importance when creating any change, and this spell is no exception. Begin by cleansing your tools with saltwater, call in your high-vibrational allies, then get crystal-clear on your intention to open yourself to receive only what is for your highest good. Standing strong in the knowledge that you are open to receive your manifestations is key. Keep in mind that there is always a path that leads to your manifestations, so allow yourself to receive guided action and inspiration that lead to your desired results.

As you light the candle, infuse it with your intention. Ask your allies to assist you with clearing any blocks to your receptivity and ask them to help you to receive fully according to your highest good. Place your significator card in front of the candle. Light the frankincense and enter into a meditative state. Visualize the light of the candle moving toward you so that it hovers above your head. As you focus on this intention, you may feel a pressure on top of your head, on your crown chakra. Surrender to this sensation, knowing that you are bringing in more of your higher self and opening your crown chakra to strengthen your connection with the divine.

See the light burning away all blocks and resistance so that you are completely open to receiving messages, wisdom, and the guided action that will help you to realize your dreams and goals. Intend that this process continues until it is fully realized. Remain in this state for as long as you feel you need to, then close by thanking your allies and grounding (see appendix A for a full grounding meditation). Allow the candle to safely burn down and go out on its own.

A Money-Drawing Spell

Use this spell to manifest money. Best started on a Sunday or Thursday during a new or waxing moon.

What You Need:
Nine of Cups
Ten of Cups
Nine of Pentacles
Ten of Pentacles
Citrine, cleansed and charged (see page 45)
Ten coins
One green or gold candle
Pine incense
Cauldron
Clove (for wealth)
Cinnamon (for success)
Bay leaf (for prosperity)
Marker (gold, if possible)

Cleanse and purify all tools and objects you are using for this spell, washing the coins first with soap and water and then in saltwater before you begin. Arrange the tarot cards in front of the candle. Using four cards is symbolic, as the number four signifies stability and solid foundations and is also associated with the archangels. Place the citrine in the middle of the cards and arrange the coins as you wish. Cast a circle (see appendix B), call in your high-vibrational allies, then state your reason for this magical working as you light the candle, infusing it with your intention and the desired outcome.

Light the pine incense and ask that it bring you money and wealth. Be as specific as possible; if you have a certain amount of money that you would like to receive, request it now. Sprinkle the clove and cinnamon in the cauldron; how much you use is up to you. With the marker, write your request on the bay leaf. You can write a certain dollar amount, or simply write *prosperity, money,* or *wealth* while visualizing what that manifested state looks like, and feels like, for you. Find the feeling of prosperity, then light the bay leaf and drop it into the cauldron. Say the following three times:

From this leaf
Burned by fire
Manifests
My desire
Money, riches
Come to me
So it is
And blessed be.

When this is done, place the lid on the cauldron and leave it undisturbed until your intention manifests. Allow the candle to burn out on its own and close as you wish. When you are ready, you can ground your energy (see appendix A for a full grounding meditation) and close the circle.

Chapter 9
September: The Harvest Moon

The Harvest Moon, while it falls in October every three years, is the name given to the full moon closest to the autumnal equinox—Mabon in Pagan traditions. It is also sometimes referred to as the Corn Moon, the Chrysanthemum Moon, the Barley Moon, or the Vine Moon. The moon is so named because of its bright light, which was a benefit to farmers as they harvested the last crops of summer.

The Harvest Moon tarot spreads included in this chapter explore what is ready to be harvested, where it is most beneficial to shift your focus, gaining spiritual illumination, what is ready to be released, where you should clear clutter, and ideal opportunities for you to create change.

The spells and rituals in this chapter include a harvest moon ritual, manifesting spiritual illumination, and a spell to restore balance and harmony to any area of your life that needs it.

An Interview with Tarot Reader Sebastian Åkesson

Sebastian Åkesson, or Father of Wands, as he is known in the online sphere, is a tarot reader and intuitive based in Sweden whose guidance and insight I have found particularly valuable over time. Following is his response to a series of questions I asked him about his practice and how he came to it. I was particularly interested in knowing more about this aspect of him because of the timeless, deep wisdom he so consistently offers.

In my opinion, the true purpose and power of tarot lies in its ability to create connection and act as a relational tool of storytelling—something which always has been, and as far as I can tell, always will be an integral part of being human. The highest value tarot provides is as a key to personal, and ultimately collective, transformation for the better. It's also a great tool for seekers of inspiration to unlock the subconscious mind and imagination, for the practice of daily meditations, expansion of the conscious mind, and for baring deeper insights.

The great numbers of decks available also provide a historical pictorial library of deep knowledge handed down through the generations. The artwork of different decks can be very gripping; it tugs at the soul strings of your being and there's a deep connection to be found in the imagery that, essentially, is a distillation of collective subconscious energies translated into images and symbols. The span and depth of interpretation—from the everyday mundane and profane to the loftiest of ideals and spiritual ideas—that can be extracted from each card is profound. There are layers upon layers of meaning in the images and symbols that stretch back throughout our evolutionary history, and there's always something new to learn and discover.

I still haven't fully explored the entirety of the reasons I gravitated toward the metaphysical, but to me, it seems part of it is rooted in the deep collective unconscious and cultural evolutionary history that permeates each and every one of us, and some of it is due to personal memories and experiences. I still remember the long dark nights of childhood growing up in the frozen north of Scandinavia, when my mum and I used to pray at night before bedtime. I remember lighting a candle, putting my hands together in prayer, and closing my eyes. This always struck a deep chord in the innermost part of my being and I think, since then, I have always known there was something bigger out there, the magic of the universe.

I'm also incredibly interested in the intuitive aspect of tarot and its interpretation, something that is highly personal and available to all who wish to pursue and try their hand at it. The cards, in having so many layers of meaning and deep complexity, connect with different people in different ways. As such, any number of varied interpretations and actionable utility can be derived from them and still be viable and highly meaningful on the personal journey of each individual. The messages from the cards can unlock your subconscious mind and allow images, feelings, and energies to surface to the conscious mind; within that there's real and tangible potential for change, growth, and transformation. The tarot provides the manifest bridge between your conscious and subconscious mind, between your spirit and your higher self.

I read tarot to make a positive and lasting difference in people's lives, to inspire constructive change, tangible growth, and ultimately, personal transformation and transcendence. Personally, I've found that the guidance and direction provided by the cards can be an invaluable asset, and I want to be able to give that to others who might be searching for hope.

Spreads

Welcoming the Harvest

The energies of the autumnal equinox support fruition and beckon the fullness of life into being, manifestations ready for harvest. Seeds planted in the past sometimes surprise us by showing up long after we have forgotten about them. Other times, they manifest into our lives much more rapidly. This spread (see illustration 9-1) helps shed light on what is ready for you to receive now and what is coming into your life in the very near future.

Suggested questions:

1. What harvest is ready for me?
2. How can I fully receive it?
3. How can I make the most of it?
4. What blessings does this harvest bring?
5. What have I sown that I will soon reap?
6. How can I ensure its full potential?
7. How will I know when it is ready?
8. A message from my guides.

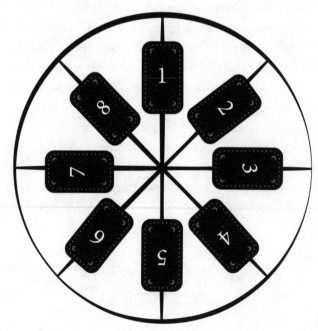

Illustration 9-1: Welcoming the Harvest

Shifting Your Focus

As the end of summer ushers in the energies of a new season, a shift takes place that heralds a change in our own priorities. Nights become longer and the landscape comes alive with a rich pageantry of color as we turn our attention homeward, to the comforts of the hearth and joyous celebrations with friends and family. Use this spread (see illustration 9-2) to examine where it would benefit you to shift your focus, whether that is to spend more time with loved ones or to take the next step in that idea you've been mulling over.

Suggested questions:

1. What shifts are taking place for me now?
2. Where would it benefit me to make adjustments?
3. Where would it benefit me to focus at this time?
4. Where should I change direction?
5. What actions should I take?
6. What energies are supporting me?
7. What is my next best step?

Illustration 9-2: Shifting Your Focus

Spiritual Illumination

Fall is a wonderful time to reflect. Whether you feel most contemplative taking in the colorful autumn scenery, meditating, making art, or through some other endeavor, in moments of alignment—those times we feel most at peace and connected to ourselves—we can gain perspective as we honor our journey thus far. From that place of clarity we can consider how to integrate the lessons and wisdom we have learned along the way. This spread (see illustration 9-3) can be used as a springboard for deeper insight and reflection.

Suggested questions:

1. What can I learn from my past?
2. What wisdom do I need to integrate?
3. How can I best accomplish this?
4. A card that reflects my current spiritual state.
5. What is my current journey meant to teach me?
6. What lessons do I still need to learn?
7. Where is my current path leading me?
8. A card representing my highest path.
9. Guidance from the universe.
10. Guidance from my inner being.
11. A message from my guides.

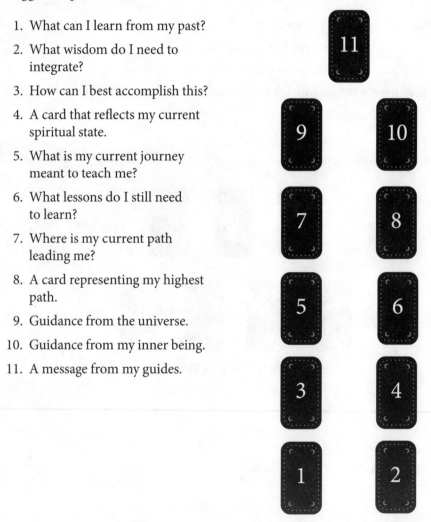

Illustration 9-3: Spiritual Illumination

What Is Ready to Be Released

Equinoxes are powerful times of shifting energies, as the transition from one season into another marks the beginning of a fresh cycle. As the old gives way to the new, we also benefit by considering how we can welcome these beginnings in support of their greatest possible outcome. This spread (see illustration 9-4) can help you to gain perspective on what should be released in order to best allow the new energies to take root.

Suggested questions:

1. What needs to be released from my life?
2. What will this release make room for?
3. How can I fully release it?
4. How can I best welcome in the new energies?
5. What changes will these new energies bring?

Illustration 9-4: What Is Ready to Be Released

Clearing Clutter

When our lives are cluttered—whether the clutter is emotional, mental, or physical—things of importance can be crowded out. On a physical level, clearing out what you no longer use and either fixing or discarding things that are broken improves the energy flow and the overall feeling of a space, which is a tenet of feng shui. On a mental level, releasing habits of thinking that aren't serving you makes room for positive replacements. Emotionally, we can become cluttered with too many unprocessed emotions, which can affect our relationships, both with others and with ourselves. Use this spread (see illustration 9-5) to gain clarity on where you need to clear clutter and how doing so will help you.

Suggested questions:

1. Where do I need to clear emotional clutter?

2. Where do I need to clear mental clutter?

3. Where do I need to clear physical clutter?

4. What is taking too much of my time?

5. What is taking too much of my energy?

6. What relationships do I need to reassess?

7. How will clearing clutter impact me?

8. What will this make room for?

9. What is my overall guidance?

Illustration 9-5: Clearing Clutter

DECLARATIONS

Many cultures and belief systems hold that words have power. Before there were written words, everything was spoken. Oral traditions passed on their stories and wisdom through the generations. Similar to writing, speaking words aloud gives them power. Just as our thoughts create our realities and inform our vibratory stance, we can also harness the power of the spoken word during rituals as well as in daily life.

Speaking your intentions and mantras in rituals in a firm, clear voice and with confidence amplifies what you are saying to the universe. The feeling of empowerment is essential to manifestation, and as physical beings, it is sometimes easier for us to feel more empowered by spoken words, as they underscore our intentions. You could think of the spoken word as an added vibration that projects your intentions through sound waves while your thoughts support that vibration as you broadcast your will to the universe.

Opportunities for Change

As the leaves all around us transform from green to a vast spectrum ranging from vibrant yellow to russet, the energies supporting those transformations are also available to us. We are seasonal creatures as much as any living being on the planet, and the rhythms of our lives flow with the cycles of the earth as the Wheel of the Year turns. This spread (see illustration 9-6) can help you to understand what is ready to shift in your life and where you can take guided action.

Suggested questions:

1. Where is change needed in my life?
2. What can I do to create the change?
3. How will making this change help me?
4. What is my first step?
5. What results will this bring about?
6. What opportunities are available to me at this time?
7. What energies are supporting me in creating these changes?

Illustration 9-6: Opportunities for Change

Spells & Rituals

Harvest Moon Ritual

This Mabon ritual allows you to honor the God and Goddess and express your gratitude, clear energies, and seed intentions for the season ahead. Best performed during the Harvest Moon.

What You Need:

Something to write with

Three sheets of paper

Chalice

Wine or apple cider (for offering)

Apple, cut horizontally to reveal the shape of a pentagram (for offering)

Gathered objects from nature, such as acorns, seed pods, pinecones, evergreen (for offering)

Cauldron

At Mabon, as one season passes into the next, we recognize the transformation as a time of bounty cedes to a period of death, making way for the renewal that will later follow. This is a time to honor the abundance we have enjoyed as well as the gifts the coming months will bring. In Pagan traditions, the God (associated with the sun) departs to return to the womb of the Goddess, who is associated with the night and darkness, a metaphor for the womb or the soil, where a seed must descend into darkness in order to prepare for later growth.

This ritual is best performed outside under the moon; if this is not possible, you can do it indoors near a window where you can see the moon. Once you gather your materials, begin by making three lists, each on a separate piece of paper. The first, a gratitude list, should include everything you are thankful for. The second, a clearing list, includes everything that isn't coming with you into the next season, which you intend to release from your life during this ritual. On the third list, you are seeding your intentions by writing down anything you want to see develop in the coming months.

Ground (see appendix A for a full grounding meditation) with the intention of releasing everything you wrote on your clearing list and send all energies that do not serve your highest good into the earth to be neutralized. Cast a circle (see appendix B) and welcome the God, honoring him for all he has provided in the season of abundance and throughout the year. Present him with the offering of acorns, evergreens, and the other natural objects you have gathered.

Next, welcome the Goddess to the circle, thanking her for her life-giving energies and for all she provides. You can, of course, tailor what you say to the God and Goddess, honoring them as you feel is appropriate. Present the Goddess with the offering of the apple by placing it on the earth or on your altar. Pour the wine or cider from the chalice onto the earth for her, or keep it on your altar if you are working indoors and pour it onto the earth after the ceremony. State your intention and ask for the support of the God and Goddess during this ritual; you can be as specific in your request as you like, but it is most effective if you are clear and direct.

State everything you are thankful for, and feel into the gratitude as fully as possible. You can bury your gratitude list in the earth if you are working outside or, if indoors, you can burn it in the cauldron to release its energies to the universe. (It may be helpful if you roll your lists into a scroll before burning them.) Next, take your clearing list and state everything you wish to release, then burn or bury it. Finally, gather your intentions list and state clearly everything you wish to see manifested in your life in the coming months. Burn or bury this and visualize, as you do so, all of your intentions coming into being as you release them into the universe.

You may choose to meditate at this point and commune with the God and Goddess before thanking and releasing them. Thank any other allies, ground, and close the circle. Scatter the ashes from the cauldron onto the earth. If you are working outside, leave the offerings on the earth; if you are working indoors, you can leave them there as long as you like, provided you dispose of them before they start to turn.

The Illumination of Spirit

Establish a stronger connection with your higher self. Best performed on a Sunday during a new, waxing, or full moon.

What You Need:
Two white Candles
Saltwater
Olive or other oil
Quartz crystal, cleansed and charged (see page 45)

For this ritual, you can choose a piece of quartz that you will wear as a necklace or to use in meditation; what is most important is that you trust your intuition when choosing the crystal. Dress your candles by cleansing them with saltwater then anointing them with an oil of your choosing; olive oil is fine for this purpose. While you dress each candle, infuse it with the intention of connecting with your higher wisdom and receiving spiritual illumination, enlightenment, and understanding. Two candles are used in this spell, one representing you and the other representing your higher self. As the lighting of a candle in ritual symbolizes the welcoming in of spirit, in lighting them both, you will be symbolically drawing your higher wisdom to you and bridging a stronger connection with your divine being.

Ground (see appendix A for a full grounding meditation), cast a circle (see appendix B), and call on your high-vibrational allies to assist you, if you wish. The first candle symbolizes your higher self, your divine Source or inner being. Light this candle and say:

I honor my higher self
And invoke its wisdom
To fill my being
On every level.

Light the second candle from the flame of the first and envision the transfer of its light illuminating you with divine knowledge as you connect powerfully with your higher self. Say:

Light of my Source
Illuminate my mind
To receive higher knowledge
And wisdom divine.

Hold the quartz over the two flames, above them at a central point, so that it absorbs the light of each one. Because quartz holds energy, you are imprinting the energy of unity between you and your higher self. As you do this, visualize the light of the two flames converging upward into a point and meeting in the crystal. Hold the intention of a powerful convergence between you and your higher self, as you create a connection that will always remain strong.

Once you have charged the quartz fully (use your intuition to tell you when this is done), you can use it during meditation or as a talisman that helps you connect with your divine being. Know, however, that this ritual has already forged a powerful connection and that the quartz can be used as support and empowerment. Think of it as an ally that assists you in strengthening the connection, which will grow over time with practice, focus, and intention. After charging the quartz, spend time in meditation, holding or wearing it as you allow yourself to receive any wisdom or messages from your higher self. When you are ready, you can ground your energy and close the circle.

Eventually, you will need to cleanse and charge the quartz; use your intuition to tell you when this needs to be done. After cleansing and recharging it, you may choose to repeat this ritual or simply infuse the crystal again with your intention so that it helps you connect with your higher self whenever you hold it or wear it.

A Balancing of the Scales

Restore balance and harmony to your life. Best performed on a Tuesday or Saturday during a half moon.

What You Need:
Your significator card

One or more of the Two pip cards (i.e., Two of Wands)

Black tourmaline or smoky quartz (to clear negative energy), cleansed and charged (see page 45)

One white candle

While it is possible to be busy and aligned, there are times when certain areas of your life can be thrown out of balance. This is a spell to restore order and harmony. The Two card or cards you choose will depend on where in your life you are seeking to establish balance (see page 7 for details on what each suit represents). You may also choose to bring in the Justice card if it aligns with your intentions.

Begin by placing the tarot cards next to each other in front of you, setting up your space as you wish, and casting a protective circle (see appendix B). Focus your attention above your head, visualizing a beam of high-vibrational divine white light descending from the heavens into your soul star chakra. Draw the white light column into you, visualizing it descending through your chakras as it clears and transmutes any blocks and energies that need to be cleared and released, including any hooks, barbs, streamers, cords, anchors, connections, and attachments.

See this light moving from your soul star into your crown, then into your third eye, throat chakra, heart chakra, solar plexus, sacral chakra, and root chakra. Feel your chakras aligning and focus on the intention that they are perfectly clear, aligned, connected, and balanced. Throughout this process, as the energies clear, you may feel the clarity as lightness in your heart center or as sensations throughout your chakras. Notice any areas where the light seems to pause and allow it to take its time as it works on restoring balance to those areas. You may sense this as a lightening or cooling sensation, as shivers, or chills; the experience is different for everyone. Remain in this state until you feel the alignment.

Hold the crystal in your receiving hand (your non-dominant hand) and ground (see appendix A for a full grounding meditation) with the intention of clearing from your mind, body, and vibration all energies that do not serve you. Clear, release, and transmute all harmful, negative, and unwanted attachments and energies of all forms that are not in alignment with your highest good; you can do this by simply intending it and visualizing it happening. If you wish, you can call on your high-vibrational allies to assist with this clearing. The angels wonderfully support this, especially Archangel Michael; you can call on him to cut away and clear all cords of attachment and energies of all forms that do not serve you, and to transmute (heal) them. Feel these energies leaving you, know that they are transmuted, and welcome in healing light of whatever color feels appropriate for you (see page 20 for color correspondences). Visualize this light surrounding you in a protective sphere.

Place the Two card or cards you have selected over your significator card, and place the crystal on top. Light the candle and visualize the parts of your life you are bringing into balance entering into a state of harmony. See the outcome you wish to manifest, then state your intention clearly in your own words. Finish by repeating the following three times:

Balance and harmony
Now reign supreme
Bringing in order
Clarity and peace
All is well and good for me
So it is and blessed be.

When you are ready, ground your energy and close the circle.

Chapter 10
OCTOBER: THE HUNTER MOON

Known instead as the Harvest Moon every three years, the Hunter Moon falls during a time of year when people busied themselves hunting and preserving meats in preparation for the winter months ahead. This moon is sometimes called the Dying Grass Moon, the Travel Moon, the Shedding Moon, or the Sanguine Moon.

The Hunter Moon tarot spreads included in this chapter examine what would be most fruitful for you to pursue, where you should be proactive, what would benefit from preparation, a glimpse into the near future, and where further exploration would pay off.

The spells and rituals in this chapter include reaping rewards for work well done, connecting with a loved one who has crossed over, and a vision quest to connect with a spirit animal.

Oracle Cards

Oracle cards are often used as supplementary tools to tarot readings, and they can be used on their own to provide a certain type of wisdom. Where most tarot decks include seventy-eight cards and are structured around the major and minor arcana, oracle decks vary in terms of the number of cards they include and in the way they are structured.

Oracle decks tend to focus on particular themes, which can vary widely and encompass subjects like Jungian archetypes, animals, or flowers, to name a few, and many of them are also designed to offer specific advice, based on subjects like love, for example. The cards will have their own guidance to impart depending on the deck. Much like selecting a tarot deck, when choosing an oracle deck, it is ideal to trust your instinct to guide you to the one that is right for you.

Tori Hartman, the creator of a chakra-focused oracle deck, writes that "Oracle cards are about breaking patterns. They often reveal to us our path to manifesting" (Hartman, 2020). They can also speak to where we are on a spiritual level, inform us of our current vibrational or emotional state, and let us know where we are headed on our experiential journey. Where tarot cards resonate with archetypal symbols that represent the essence of timeless life situations and experiences, oracle cards can be useful for helping us to navigate certain frames of mind and to understand on a deeper, more personal level where we need to create shifts

to achieve our desired results, providing us with guidance that resonates with us specifically.

There are many ways to use oracle cards in concert with a tarot reading. One method is to draw an oracle card before beginning a reading to provide a picture of the querent's emotional state, challenges, or whatever you deem the card to represent. Much like choosing a card in response to a particular question during a tarot reading, choose or have the querent choose the question to ask before drawing the oracle card. This could be anything from *What represents my current emotional state?* to *What internal challenges am I facing now?* to *What shifts do I need to make to accomplish my goals?* This card will set the tone for the tarot reading and can be a useful reference point to link the interpretation of the remaining cards in the reading.

An oracle card can also stand as the theme for the reading overall. You can select it either at the end or the beginning of the tarot reading, depending on your preference. With this method, the tarot cards that emerge in the reading may provide a more complete picture of what the oracle card represents, so that its meaning becomes fully clear at the end. In this way, an oracle card can illuminate a situation and its underlying energies in a sometimes visceral way that reaches to the heart of a reading.

Repeating Cards

Sometimes you will see certain cards come up for you again and again. There can be several reasons for this. Repeating cards may have certain meanings to impart to you that you haven't fully grasped, or they could be attempting to shed light on particular aspects of a situation that you aren't clearly seeing.

It could be that such a card represents something on its way to you that has been attempting to reach you for a while. It could be taking its time in getting there, or it is available to you but you are blocking it in some way, whether through resistant thoughts or beliefs that are holding it at arm's length and preventing it from fully manifesting or reaching you. There are other reasons cards can repeat, such as to indicate something that is taking a while to build, but that it is continuing to grow.

Repeating cards can also be intended as powerful symbols that are entering your awareness as reminders. A recurring Strength card, for example, could be reminding you of your inner power or urging you to tap into your strength and build upon it. Tune in to your intuition, or use a pendulum to ask yes or no questions so you can gain clarity on what the card is trying to tell you. You can also ask further questions of your tarot deck to achieve a better understanding of the card's message.

Spreads

The Thrill of the Hunt

Life is filled with opportunities—more than we can feasibly pursue. Use this spread (see illustration 10-1) to help you narrow down possibilities and guide you toward a particular path, the one that promises to bear the most fruit. You can tailor your questions to be specific to anything you are asking for help on, whether it is related to career, education, or relationships. As with any tarot reading, it is a good idea to focus on your situation or question before beginning, as this will help provide more meaningful results.

Suggested questions:

1. A card representing the supporting energies behind the situation.
2. Which path will lead me to my best outcome?
3. What are my first steps?
4. What actions should I take to see me through?
5. Where am I supported along the way?
6. What is my ultimate destination?
7. Advice from my higher self.

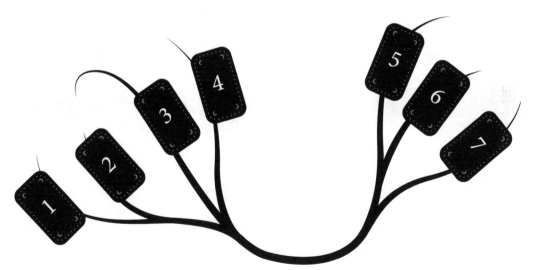

Illustration 10-1: The Thrill of the Hunt

Paving the Way

Much of the time, we can ensure better results from being proactive, and planning ahead for the future can save time (and sometimes expense, either energetic or financial) later on. But it can be easy for things to slip through the cracks; you *thought* you had taken care of X, and then Y happened. This is a good check-in spread (see illustration 10-2), especially when you are busy and have major undertakings, changes, or projects about to take place.

Suggested questions:

1. What situation would benefit from pre-paving?
2. What aspects need further planning?
3. What needs more structure?
4. What steps am I advised to take now?
5. What especially needs my attention?
6. What do I need to take a closer look at?
7. Something I need to make sure doesn't get forgotten.
8. How can I ensure the best results?

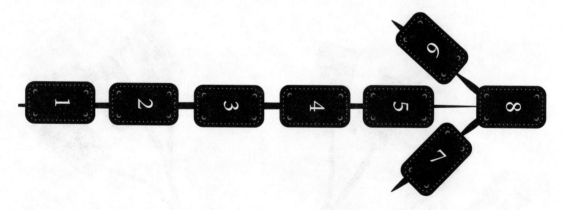

Illustration 10-2: Paving the Way

Making Preparations

Just as we make preparations when the weather turns cooler, getting ready for the season ahead, we also prepare physically when we are moving house, emotionally when situations begin to change, and spiritually when we are healing, experiencing energetic shifts, or working through any challenges life may bring. This spread (see illustration 10-3) can be tailored to your specific query or situation and is especially useful in illuminating the nature of shifts that are taking place around you and revealing how you can navigate the changes with ease.

Suggested questions:

1. A card representing the energies of the situation.
2. A card representing the preparations that need to be made.
3. How can I best prepare?
4. What aspects should not be ignored?
5. What aspects are shifting?
6. Where am I supported?
7. What actions am I advised to take?
8. What result will these actions have?
9. What changes can I make to support the best possible outcome?
10. Advice from my guides.

Illustration 10-3: Making Preparations

A Look Ahead

This is a great all-purpose spread (see illustration 10-4) that you can use when you simply want to take a peek into the near future to see what is coming—generally from now through the next three to six months—or if you have a specific question or situation in mind and you are curious what the outcome will be if things continue along on their current path.

Suggested questions:

1. What is on the horizon for me?
2. What will this bring?
3. What do I need to know about it?
4. Where will it lead?
5. What is its purpose?
6. What actions should I take now?
7. Advice from the universe.

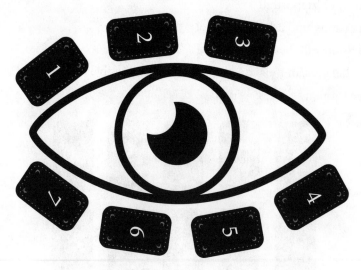

Illustration 10-4: A Look Ahead

CRYSTAL ACTIVATION

Crystals are powerful allies. They are physical expressions of earth energy that vibrate at different frequencies to support us through their particular energetic attributes. Sitting with a crystal in gratitude can activate it powerfully. Simply hold a crystal that has been cleansed and charged (see page 45) and be with it, feeling gratitude for its partnership and support. Send it love and thank it through your vibration for its assistance. If you can sense energy, you may notice heat or a warm sensation emanating from the crystal, or you may be able to feel its vibration pulsating in your hand. Activating crystals before working with them brings forth their highest attributes and adds potency to any meditation, healing, or ritual.

The Road Less Traveled

To take the road less traveled requires an adventurous spirit, and sometimes the adventure is more important than the destination itself. There is a common saying, *the joy is in the journey*, that applies here. We often take vacations to get away into something new, for the experiences we will have along the way, relishing the potential for excitement and the new people and places to be encountered. Taking the less trodden path can result in fortunate encounters, joyous happenstance, and life-changing discoveries. Use this spread (see illustration 10-5) to reveal where you would benefit from stepping outside of norms and traditions or departing from the usual.

Suggested questions:

1. Where am I being guided to make an unconventional choice?
2. What would benefit from my further exploration?
3. Why should I pursue this?
4. How will this help me?
5. Where should I begin?
6. What direction will this take me?
7. Where will it ultimately lead?
8. Where do I need to dig a little deeper?
9. Advice from my guides.
10. Advice from my higher self.

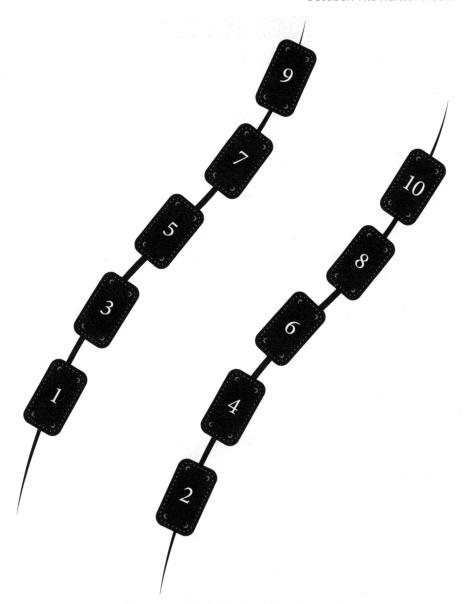

Illustration 10-5: The Road Less Traveled

Spells & Rituals

Reaping Rewards

Use this mantra to call in the good things that are ready to enter your life. Best performed on a Sunday during a full moon.

While this simple spell is ideally aligned with the energies on a Sunday during a full moon, this is a mantra you can use anytime you want to call something to you. If nothing comes, it is most likely still in preparation or it isn't ready to manifest yet. You can repeat this incantation on a regular basis to keep calling it to you. Just make sure you are not blocking it with any resistant beliefs or thoughts that work against it; if you are, you will benefit from some inner work to clear out the blocks. Note any guided action steps that come into your awareness, as these may be nudges from your inner being to steer you in the direction of receiving what you are asking for.

Repeat three times:

All good things due to me
Come to me soon
All money and messages
Blessings and boons
Abundance that is mine
Comes in due time
Success and prosperity
Now come to me
By the light of the moon
Rewards come soon.

On the third repetition, end the incantation with: *So it is and blessed be.*

Making Contact

Make contact with someone who has crossed over. Best performed on Samhain, a Monday or Saturday, or during the dark moon.

What You Need:
A large bowl of water or a black mirror
One black candle
One white candle
Sea salt

Frankincense resin or incense
Obsidian, tourmaline, or smoky quartz, cleansed and charged (see page 45)
Kyanite or apophyllite, cleansed and charged (see page 45)
A photo of the person you are trying to contact and/or something that belonged to
   them

First, gather your supplies. Whether you use a bowl of water or a black mirror is entirely up to you; just make sure to physically cleanse and energetically purify the bowl or mirror with the method of your choosing before beginning, then focus your intentions on the water, if you are using it, that it serves as a potent ally for bridging the connection during this ritual. The black candle is for protection, and the white candle represents connection with spirit. There are many crystals you can choose for protection, but obsidian, tourmaline, and smoky quartz are among the most common. You can use a combination of these and add any additional crystals as you feel guided. Kyanite and apophyllite aid in communication with the spiritual realms.

Before casting the circle, make sure all of your tools are cleansed, purified, and within easy reach. Set up the photo of the person you are making contact with and any personal effects behind the bowl of water or black mirror. The candles should be on either side of the mirror or bowl, with the crystals in front of it and the frankincense nearby. This is ideally performed in a darkened room with no artificial lights on.

When attempting to connect with someone who has crossed over, a certain measure of caution is in order. For this ritual, make sure you cast a circle (see appendix B) to protect yourself from unwanted and unwelcome energies and call on the archangels and high-vibrational allies for added protection. It is also recommended to call the quarters and welcome in the guardians (see appendix B to reference the invocations and devocations). Before casting the circle, ground your energy (see appendix A for a full grounding meditation), raise your vibration, and create an unbroken line of salt in a circle all around you. Do not step or reach outside of the salt circle or break the line until the ritual is done and you have released the quarters, thanked your allies, and closed the circle.

Light the incense first, thanking the angels and allies for their protection and assistance. Ask your allies and the guardians to ensure that only the person you intend to contact comes through, only if they are available, and only if it is permitted according to your highest good. Light the black candle, stating that it protects you during this ritual and allows in only the person you intend to contact (state their name and look at their photo or hold the image of them in your mind). Light the white candle and state the person's name. Ask them if they are available to speak with you. If the candle goes out, the answer is no, and you can close the circle and end the ritual. If it continues to burn or the flame burns brighter, the answer is yes.

If you are using a bowl of water, gaze softly at the flames reflected on the surface of the water. Continue to meditate on the water and notice any ripples or shadows that move across its surface. If you are using a black mirror, gaze at the reflection of the flames on the surface of the glass and notice any changes in the reflection as the candlelight flickers across it. You may begin to feel the person's presence. Ask them any questions you have and talk to them as you normally would, as if they were sitting in front of you. You can continue to gaze at the surface of the water or glass or meditate for as long as you feel called to.

When you are done, thank the person and send them love, then tell them goodbye. Remember that you can always contact them again or attempt to contact them whenever you like, but always be extremely cautious when performing this ritual and ensure that you always call in your high-vibrational allies for support and protection as mentioned above. After thanking your angels and allies, releasing the quarters, grounding, and closing the circle, you can step outside of or break the salt line.

Finding Your Spirit Animal: A Vision Quest

Discover your spirit animal and gain clarity on any messages it has for you. This ritual can be performed at any time.

What You Need:
One white or green candle
Incense of your choosing (optional)
Journal and/or sketchbook

This quest can be performed indoors or outside. If you are performing it indoors, set aside time and space where you will have privacy and can work in a peaceful environment. If outside noises are an issue, you can use headphones to listen to soothing, high-vibrational music (preferably instrumental so you are not distracted by lyrics). However, you may have a more meaningful experience if you do this outside in nature, in an area where you will not be disturbed for a long period of time. Only use the candle and incense if you are performing this indoors.

Traditionally, vision quests were a rite of passage marking the transition from childhood to adulthood. The person would be sent out into the wild or enclosed in a designated area for a fasting period of two to four days, during which they would receive a visitation of an animal guide in a dream or vision. A vision quest in the natural world may not yield results in a single day—this may entail repeated visitations.

If you are venturing out in nature, you may choose to go for a long walk or find a place to sit and meditate. Take note of any feathers, fur, or other objects you find along the way that feel significant to you. Observe any animal that crosses your path or that is brought to your attention. A bird may fly in front of you or directly overhead, or an animal could quite literally cross your path. You may simply find yourself turning to look at a certain spot for no reason you can discern and see the animal that is meant for you.

The first animal you see won't necessarily hold significance for you; trust your instinct. If you are drawn to a certain area, follow your inner wisdom. If you find yourself making eye contact with an animal, this is significant. If you can't identify the species, take note of any distinguishing characteristics and markings. You may want to take a picture of it or sketch it right away so memory doesn't erase its features. Feel into the messages and wisdom the animal has for you. This may be guidance in the form of your mission or purpose, or information that will help you in other areas of your life.

If you are doing this indoors as a ritual, cast a circle (see appendix B) and call on your high-vibrational allies. Light the incense and the candle, using the flame as a point of connection with your animal guide. State the intention that you wish to connect with your spirit animal, then enter a deep state of meditation and tune in to any visions you receive. This may be an extended meditation in which you go deep within. Depending on your abilities, you may see or perceive an animal in your mind's eye, or even hear a specific animal sound.

Once you have identified your animal, ask what message it is meant to impart to you. Record any observations and information you receive in a journal. When you are ready, you can ground your energy (see appendix A for a full grounding meditation) and close the circle. After you have ended the ritual, further investigation of your animal guide's symbolism may prove enlightening.

Following the ritual, you may see the animal appear in photographs, symbols, and other imagery you encounter in everyday life. Once you have identified what this animal is here to teach you, every time you see it, whether in real life or in imagery, you may begin to gain a deeper understanding of the meaning it is meant to impart to you. It can be a message to stay strong or to tune in to your inner wisdom, to name just a few examples. Observing your thoughts and what is going on at the time you see your animal guide can be illuminating, as it may hold a message directly related to what you are thinking or experiencing at the time that you see it.

Chapter 11

NOVEMBER: THE BEAVER MOON

Named for the creatures that spring into action preparing their lodges for winter, the Beaver Moon is also sometimes referred to as the Frost Moon, the Tree Moon, or the Trading Moon.

The spreads included in this chapter guide you to take a look at where and how you can be more productive, how to create more stability in a situation, bolstering your foundations for improved strength and longevity, strengthening your sense of security, clearing blocks, and a work and career spread.

The spells and rituals in this chapter include summoning the perfect career opportunity, creating solid financial foundations, and a road opener spell to pave the way for your future success.

Animal Symbolism in Tarot

When a certain animal appears for you again and again, take heed. The universe may be communicating to you through use of an archetype or symbol. Birds can be messengers, bears and lions often stand for strength and power, and foxes are allied with quickness and cunning, for example. In tarot, you will often feel the resonance of certain animals, just as you feel drawn to them in daily life. Butterflies, while they are insects and not strictly considered animals, as members of the natural world are powerful messengers and make their appearance on various cards throughout many tarot decks.

If you already have an animal, plant, or insect you feel a connection with, you may find that it appears for you in tarot readings in answer to your questions or that it appears around you at significant times in your life. Along with reoccurring numbers, these envoys from the world around us are one way our nonphysical support network and our allies send us messages—whether they are emblems of strength, transformation, encouragement, or better times ahead.

Spreads

A Look at Productivity

An important part of maximizing efficiency is pausing to regroup, reassess, and reorganize. When we take time to gather our thoughts and examine our processes—whether for work and career, creative projects, or in some other area of life—it gives us a chance to clarify what remains to be done and consider how we can best accomplish those tasks with optimal results. This spread (see illustration 11-1) can help you gain clarity on specific projects and undertakings, and it is also useful in taking a closer look at where you would benefit from reordering your priorities.

Suggested questions:

1. Where would I benefit from being more productive?
2. Where are my efforts best applied?

3. Where do I need to expend less energy?

4. How can I maximize my potential?

5. What approach should I take to accomplish this?

6. How will this benefit me overall?

7. Where do I need to pause?

8. What do I need to reexamine?

9. What do I need to reorganize?

10. How can I achieve the greatest possible outcome?

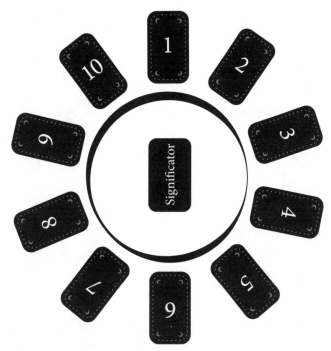

Illustration 11-1: A Look at Productivity

Creating Stability

Whether you are looking ahead at an impending life change, in the midst of one, or sitting in its aftermath, use this spread to tune in to universal energies and receive guidance on how to stabilize a situation, and how to lend strength and solidity to certain areas of your life that are new or shifting or that could simply benefit from some shoring up. This spread (see illustration 11-2) can be used in concert with the spread that follows. Where this spread looks at stabilizing a certain situation, the next spread dives into creating and strengthening foundations for the long term.

Suggested questions:

1. What area of my life would benefit from being more stable?
2. How can I create this stability?
3. What is my first step?
4. What energies are available to support me?
5. What energies are supporting the stability?
6. Where do I need to shift my perspective?
7. Where should I focus to support my endeavors?
8. Advice from my allies.
9. Advice from my higher self.
10. Wisdom from the universe.

Illustration 11-2: Creating Stability

Strengthening Foundations

Like beavers building dams to ensure their comfort and safety during the cooler months, we also benefit from planning ahead for our future vitality and success. This spread (see illustration 11-3) allows you to consider the foundations in your life—whether they have to do with work or business, family, relationships, finances, future endeavors, or property—and where they could use strengthening to ensure their health and stability over the long term.

If you already have a specific situation, undertaking, or relationship in mind that you want to ask about, you can replace the first question with an inquiry about the situation's current state. Note that if you receive a card like the Tower in response to where something currently stands, it may be guidance that it is best to let it crumble. Use your intuition and internal guidance to tell you when it is time it let something go, and when it would benefit you to put your energies toward strengthening it.

Suggested questions:

1. What foundations in my life need strengthening?
2. A card representing the current energetic strength of the situation.
3. How can I strengthen these foundations?
4. What are my challenges?
5. How can I overcome those challenges?
6. Where should I focus my efforts now?
7. What are my next best steps?
8. How can I ensure its future health and vitality?
9. How can I ensure its longevity?
10. Where am I supported?

Illustration 11-3: Strengthening Foundations

A Sense of Security

Most of us have experienced the feeling of wanting a situation to be more secure. When you start a new project, career, or relationship or when you move to a new city (to name a few examples), it is nice to have a clear picture of what you can do to ensure the success of the new situation and strengthen your place within it. This spread (see illustration 11-4) is useful for doing just that. Use it as a check-in with the universe and to gain insight and awareness of the energies of a situation or undertaking and what you can do to maximize your success.

Suggested questions:

1. What is the energetic timbre of the situation?

2. How can I create a stronger sense of security?

3. In what ways am I currently supported?

4. How can I ensure that I am supported in the future?

5. Where would I benefit from greater clarity?

6. How can I ensure the overall success of the situation?

7. How can I ensure my own success?

8. What changes can I make that will make the situation more secure?

9. How should I proceed for the best possible outcome?

10. A message from the universe.

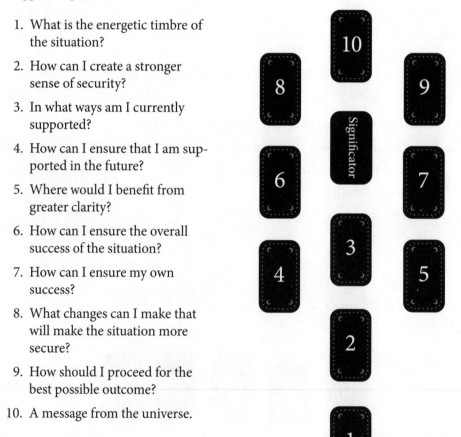

Illustration 11-4: A Sense of Security

Clearing Blocks

Whether you have been working toward something and not seeing the results you want or you simply cannot seem to move forward with it, this spread (see illustration 11-5) can provide insight on where you have blocks and how to clear them so you can begin to experience flow and momentum. There may be more than one area of your life where you are blocked, and there may be more than one block, so, of course, feel free to draw as many cards for the same question as you feel guided to. Overhand shuffling will allow multiple cards to fall out of the deck for a single question; sometimes it's good to simply let the universe deliver.

Suggested questions:

1. In what area(s) of my life am I blocked?
2. A card representing the block.
3. What is the source of this block?
4. What is the block not letting in?
5. How can I clear this block?
6. What else can I do to fully receive what is available to me?
7. Advice from my inner being.

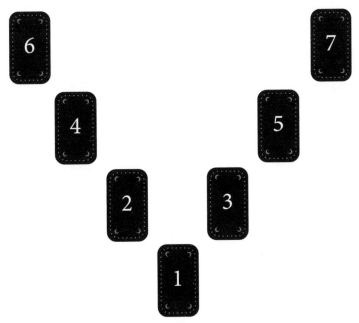

Illustration 11-5: Clearing Blocks

A Work and Career Check-In

If one thing is certain, it's change. Even when things seem to be flowing well, energies are constantly shifting. When it comes to work, there are often many people, and their intentions, collaboratively involved in influencing various aspects in the workplace. Use this spread (see illustration 11-6) to gauge where things stand in your current work environment; it is also useful if you are considering changing jobs, seeking a new job, thinking of moving into a new career, or starting a business. You can also tailor the questions so they specifically relate to your job, coworkers, and anything that may currently be going on in your workplace.

Suggested questions:

1. A card representing the overall energies of my work and career situation.
2. What changes can I make that will benefit me?
3. What advice is there for me regarding my job/career/business?
4. What is taking place behind the scenes that will affect me?
5. What do I need to be aware of?
6. What isn't working for me?
7. What is working in my favor?
8. What are my greatest skills/talents?
9. Where can I enhance my knowledge/skill set?
10. Advice from my higher self.

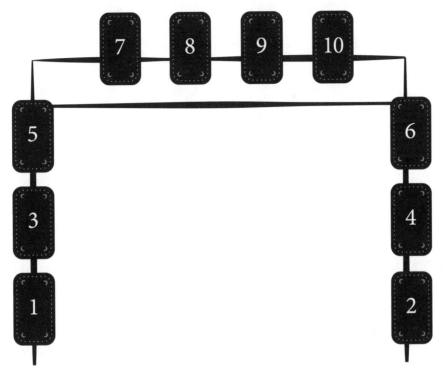

Illustration 11-6: A Work and Career Check-In

Automatic Writing

Anyone can try their hand at automatic writing; you don't necessarily have to have any special gifts or abilities to do it although, as divine beings, we are all connected to infinite intelligence. The more you are tuned in to nonphysical energy, the more information you will be able to receive. Some practitioners choose to write by hand, using pen or pencil and paper, as it is more tactile, while others prefer to use a computer so they can write more quickly and focus entirely on the message they are receiving without being distracted by the physical process of writing. The method you choose is up to you.

To begin, enter a meditative state and call on your high-vibrational allies for support and protection. Raise your vibration through any means you choose, such as music or meditation, and set the intention that you only receive information from high-vibrational energies, then ask for the messages that are meant for you to come through at this time. It might take a moment for you to get into the flow, and you can write or type your question to get you started. Note that entering a state of trust helps open you to the stream of information that is available to you.

Much like the tarot, you can ask any question you like. With practice, you will find that you are able to receive more easily and connect to what is truly an endless stream of information, knowledge, and wisdom that is always at your disposal.

Spells & Rituals

Summoning the Perfect Career Opportunity

Use this ritual to manifest a specific job or career path. Best performed on a Sunday or Wednesday during the new or waxing moon.

What You Need:

One green candle

Paper and pen (use green ink if possible)

Cauldron

Pyrite, cleansed and charged (see page 45)

Cinnamon, clove, or cinquefoil incense

Your significator card

Any tarot card(s) representing your desired career

A printed symbol of your chosen company or career field, or a printed job posting

When choosing your supporting tarot cards, you may want to choose cards that represent your level of emotional fulfillment in the career or job (such as the Ten of Cups and/or the Ace of Cups), the financial aspects (such as the Six of Pentacles and/or Nine of Pentacles), and any other cards that represent the nature of the work you will be doing, as well as additional cards you feel guided to use.

If you want to work for a certain company, you can print their logo to use for this spell. If you want to be chosen for a specific job opening, you can print the job posting. If you don't have a specific company or job in mind but want to open the way to start a career in, say, the healthcare field, you can print a related symbol such as the caduceus.

Ground your energy (see appendix A for a full grounding meditation) and create a sacred space (see appendix B). Dress and prepare the candle, carving any symbols or writing into it, such as runes, a company name or job title, something representing your chosen career field, and/or the amount of money you wish to make per year. Cleanse and charge all tools and components and set them up as you wish. You may choose to call on your high-vibrational allies; Ganesh is an ally who helps clear obstacles and ushers in success and prosperity. Burn the incense as an offering to your allies and to support the energies of abundance and opportunity. Light the candle and state your purpose for the magical working.

Write down on the paper specifically what you wish to manifest, and be as clear as possible, including things like your desired income, benefits, job title, and/or your chosen career field. Wrap or fold the paper with your written manifestation together with any images or printouts, then safely burn these in the cauldron to release their power to the universe. Place the tarot cards signifying your career over your significator card, and place the pyrite on top.

Enter a state of meditation and visualize yourself where you want to be in your career. Be specific in your visualization and feel how you will feel when you have the job or are working in the field. What does your office look like? How do you feel when you are at work? How well are you performing? Do you receive raises, promotions, and recognition? Where do you live? What kind of car are you driving? What is your relationship with your coworkers and bosses? What do you meetings look like? Are you in a leadership role?

Continue in meditation for as long as you wish, then close in gratitude, thanking any allies, grounding, and closing the circle. Come back to this visualization often to add to its momentum.

Creating Solid Financial Foundations

Create a talisman that brings you material security. Best performed on a Sunday or Thursday during the new or waxing moon.

What You Need:
Gold-colored coins (as many as you like)
A drawstring pouch or a fabric square and ribbon
Cinnamon (for success)
Clove (for wealth)
Paper and pen (green or gold, if possible)

Be sure to cleanse and purify all items you will be using before beginning (see page 45). For coins, it is a good idea to wash them with soap and water to remove surface grime, then let them sit overnight in saltwater to clear any residual energies (they pass through a lot of hands). The number of coins you use for this spell is up to you. You can also use a pre-made drawstring pouch, or create your own using a fabric square and a length of ribbon. If you choose the latter, you can stitch the fabric together or simply gather it by the corners, bunch it up at the top, then tie it around with the ribbon at the appropriate point in the spell.

Get clear on your intentions and how much money you want to ask for. Remember— the sky is the limit and you create your own reality; just be sure that you *believe* you can receive the amount you are asking for. The stronger your belief—the closer you are to knowing you will receive what you are asking for—the more powerful this spell will be. Write down the amount of money on the piece of paper and fold it into a square. You can write any sigils or symbols, such as runes, on the paper.

Place the paper in the pouch, followed by the gold coins, the cinnamon, and the clove. Tie the pouch together, creating three knots. With each knot, say, *Three times three, this money comes to me.* Before burying the pouch, say the following three times while infusing your intention into it:

> *By the dark of the moon*
> *This money is seeded*
> *Three times three*
> *My wish is heeded*
> *Wealth and money*
> *Now come to me*
> *Financial foundations*
> *And prosperity*
> *So it is*
> *And blessed be*

Find a place outside to bury your talisman. If you cannot bury it directly in the ground, you may choose a potted plant for it to share its home with. If the latter, bury it in the pot of a money-drawing variety like a jade plant, which supports the energy of prosperity. This talisman's presence in the earth is symbolic and welcomes in the supportive energies of foundational solidity and material security.

Paving the Way for Success

Call on Ganesh to assist you with clearing obstacles to your desired outcome. Best started on a Sunday, Wednesday, or Thursday during the new, waxing, or full moon.

What You Need:
Sweetgrass, cedar, or palo santo for smudging
Four black candles
Your significator card
Pyrite, cleansed and charged (see page 45)
Citrine, cleansed and charged (see page 45)

Aragonite, cleansed and charged (see page 45)

An image or statue of Ganesh

Fruits, flowers, sweets, and/or bananas for offering

Dragon's blood ink or red pen

Paper

Orange peel (for good luck and fortune)

Dragon's blood incense

This is a type of road opener spell. Before beginning, get clear on what breakthroughs you are looking to make in your life, and what situations you want to see transformed. Prepare yourself before the ceremony by taking a cleansing bath in epsom salts or sea salt, then smudge yourself with sweetgrass, cedar, or ethically sourced palo santo.

Create a sacred space and call the quarters (see appendix B), and invite any high-vibrational allies. Arrange the candles so they are in the north, east, south, and west of your altar or the space in which you are working. Place your significator card in the center of the candles, and place the pyrite, citrine, and aragonite around your card. Pyrite is a stone of protection and abundance; citrine absorbs negativity and brings clarity, joy, and wealth; and aragonite is a powerful crystal for breakthroughs. You may choose to substitute or add other crystals, depending on your intentions for this spell.

Make sure the statue of Ganesh is facing east. Welcome Ganesh and state your purpose, then place the offerings in front of him. At the top of the paper, write *Om Gam Ganapataye Namaha*. This is the mantra of Ganesh and will assist you in clearing any obstacles. Then, on the paper below the mantra, write what you wish to clear and what transformations you wish to see, then fold the paper and place it in the orange peel. If the peel is in smaller pieces, place the peel on top of the paper. Light the incense with the intention that, as it burns, it clears and releases all obstacles to what you desire; you can state your intention silently or aloud.

State the following as you light each candle, starting with the north and working your way clockwise around the quarters. Say:

In the north, I call upon the element of earth
To clear away all obstacles that hinder my progress
And welcome in abundant success.

In the east, I call upon the element of air
To clear away all obstacles that hinder my progress
And welcome in abundant success.

In the south, I call upon the element of fire
To clear away all obstacles that hinder my progress
And welcome in abundant success.

In the west, I call upon the element of water
To clear away all obstacles that hinder my progress
And welcome in abundant success.

If you work with elemental energies, you may want to include them in the above incantation as you light each candle, inviting them in to support you.

Meditate with the crystals as the candles burn down, envisioning your obstacles clearing and everything that is in your way dissolving and dissipating with ease. See yourself moving forward powerfully into the place you want to be as your desired state comes into being with ease. When you are ready, thank and release Ganesh, your allies, the quarters, and the elementals if you called them in, then ground (see appendix A for a full grounding meditation) and close the circle as usual. On the third day after the ritual, bury the orange peels in the ground together with the paper and return the offerings to the earth, thanking Ganesh again for his support.

Chapter 12
December: The Cold Moon

December's Cold Moon is aptly named for the chill that comes with the onset of winter. It is sometimes referred to as the Oak Moon, the Long Nights Moon, or the Moon Before Yule.

The Cold Moon tarot spreads included in this chapter guide you to take a look deep within, explore your subconscious mind, connect with your higher self, receive clarity on what is currently gestating in preparation for future emergence, and what lies dormant.

The spells and rituals in this chapter encompass the domains of cutting cords, healing, an energetic and auric clearing to release unwanted energies, and a house clearing and blessing.

Using Tarot to Check in with Your Vibration

When you are energetically clear—that is, free of any vibrations that are causing resistance or blocking you from your highest achievable state of being—you can magnetically and easily draw to you that which you wish to manifest in quicker time and with a resonant purity that doesn't energetically muddy the waters with anything that contradicts your desires. When your energy is clear, you are able to rise to, or vibrate at, higher frequencies, which allows you to hold more light.

When you encounter blockages and resistance, tarot can be a useful tool in helping you to discern what might be holding what you want away from you or otherwise preventing it from reaching you. To check in, sit in meditation until your mind is clear. Then hold your favorite deck and sit with it a moment while you focus on a question such as, *Where am I blocked?* or *Where am I creating resistance?* or *What is my current vibrational state?*, and be open to receiving the answer that is true and correct for you.

As you proceed on your healing journey—which is a lifelong journey for all of us, as we are continually clearing and releasing layers of energy that no longer serve us—you can check in with tarot periodically to gauge your current energy, how you are progressing, where you are vibrationally, and what needs to be cleared, released, and transmuted.

Spreads

A Look Within

During the winter months, much of the landscape lies dormant under a chill that places all the world on hold. It is a necessary pause, during which powerful transformations are taking place, unseen, in the dark and cold, buried within the womb of the earth. There is life in this latency as energies gather and strengthen in preparation for future becoming. We, as beings of nature, with bodies that respond as the tides to the pull of the moon, are energetically aligned with these seeds of becoming. Use this spread (see illustration 12-1) to check in with yourself on all levels, adding to the questions if you feel moved to do so, and to call upon the unseen forces around you for guidance, wisdom, and direction.

Suggested questions:

1. A card reflecting my current vibrational state.

2. A card reflecting my current emotional state.

3. A card reflecting my current physical state.

4. A card representing my current spiritual state.

5. Guidance from my inner being.

6. A message from my guides.

7. A message from the angelic realm.

8. Guidance from the universe.

Illustration 12-1: A Look Within

Tuning In to the Subconscious

As tarot brings forth archetypal symbols that stand in for universal experiences, the subconscious mind is attuned to these archetypes as part of the collective unconscious that holds the whole of our experience from time immemorial. We, as containers of our individual experience, carry different aspects of this knowing within ourselves, and these forces can guide us without our conscious awareness. Our subconscious mind is a powerful force that drives us, like an engine, and can function to our betterment or to our detriment. This spread (see illustration 12-2) allows you to tap into your subconscious and bring into the light what has been concealed.

Suggested questions:

1. A card representing my subconscious mind.
2. What do I need to be aware of about my subconscious?
3. What is my subconscious trying to tell me at this time?
4. What is preparing to surface from my subconscious?
5. What subconscious beliefs are not serving me?
6. What shifts do I need to make on a subconscious level?
7. How can I make these shifts?
8. What do I need to clear from my subconscious?
9. How can I go about clearing it?

Illustration 12-2: Tuning In to the Subconscious

Connecting with Your Higher Self

Just as we are guided from within by our subconscious, we are guided from without by a being larger than ourselves—our divine aspect, the being from which we are sourced. The higher self or inner being is connected to realms to which we have limited access in our three-dimensional, physical, human experience. This all-seeing, all-knowing part of ourselves can provide us with invaluable guidance and wisdom that benefits us in the achievement of our goals and the attainment of our highest good. Use this spread (see illustration 12-3) to attune to your higher wisdom, discover how you can strengthen the connection, and receive the knowledge that will most benefit you at this time.

Suggested questions:

1. What card represents my current state of connection with my higher self?

2. How can I strengthen my connection with my higher self?

3. How can I strengthen my intuition?

4. In what ways is my higher self currently guiding me?

5. A message from my higher self regarding my current life path.

6. Further guidance from my higher self.

Illustration 12-3:
Connecting with Your Higher Self

Reading Spreads Horizontally and Vertically

In spreads with more than one row, the influences of the cards on one another can be interpreted both vertically and horizontally. Consider how the meanings of the cards in each row influence one another, and then look at how the cards interface with each other in the columns. For instance, say the first row of a reading contains the Eight of Pentacles, the Sun, and the Ace of Wands. One possible interpretation of those three cards in combination could be that your hard work is going to pay off in terms of recognition—which could be a raise, promotion, award, new opportunity, or all of the above. Then, let's say the first column contains the Eight of Pentacles and beneath it, the High Priestess. You might look at this and understand the development in another light; the High Priestess could signify using your intuition in your work and letting your inner wisdom guide you. Because you followed your instinct, your hard work is bearing fruit.

A Time of Gestation

Bears enter their caves, seeds lie frozen in the earth, and all of nature grows quiet and still as it gains strength and gathers energy. Winter is as necessary as spring for the life that will emerge, as trees that experience time in the chill produce stronger, more abundant buds when the weather warms. We, too, need this time of retreat and silence, to allow ourselves time for rest and renewal; nature hints at this with the shortening of the days and lengthening of the nights, with the dropping of temperatures that send us indoors to nestle in comfort. Use this spread (see illustration 12-4) to gain clarity on what is becoming for you, hidden though it may be.

Suggested questions:

1. What is currently gestating for me?
2. What is its present status?
3. What will it become?
4. How can I nurture it at this time?
5. How can I ensure the best possible outcome?
6. How will I know when it is ready to emerge?
7. Where would I benefit from rest?

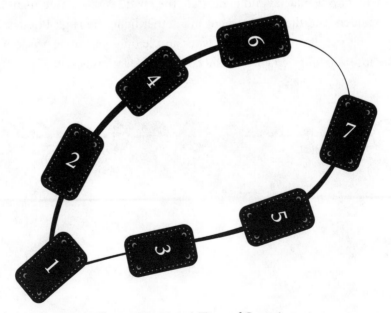

Illustration 12-4: A Time of Gestation

A Period of Dormancy

For everything there is a season, and times when we are asked to surrender in trust to the universe and allow things to arrive as they may. Many of us are doers, planners, thinkers, and so to surrender is a challenge that asks of us something we may not want to give. It is a humbling reminder that we are not in control of everything, that we live in the midst of forces greater than ourselves. When we live in alignment and flow harmoniously with the energies around us, we become more attuned to ourselves and to the guidance that is available to us. Use this spread (see illustration 12-5) to tune in to what you are being asked to shelve for now and what is being held for emergence at a later time.

Suggested questions:

1. What should I put on the back burner for now?
2. What is currently being delayed for me?
3. What is the reason for the delay?
4. How is this period of pause benefiting me?
5. How am I advised to proceed at this time?
6. Further insight from the universe.

Illustration 12-5: A Period of Dormancy

Spells & Rituals
Cutting Cords

Sever, clear, and heal connections that do not serve your highest good. Best performed on a Saturday during the waning moon.

What You Need:
Black kyanite, cleansed and charged (see page 45)
Black tourmaline, cleansed and charged (see page 45)
One white candle
Your significator card

When we cross paths with other people or energies, we can form connections that keep us tied to the person, being, energy, or situation until we sever the connection. If the experience was unpleasant, it is a good idea to make a clean break. Sometimes we release connections without being consciously aware of it, as a natural result of the parting of ways, through our own unconscious processes of healing, or through work we do on a soul level, sometimes in the dream state. Other times, we need to release these energies consciously and intentionally.

With some connections, especially those that are unhealthy or that caused you grief, it is important to clear the energy so you can move on. If you feel drained, depleted, or low on energy when you are around someone, it could be a sign that they are siphoning your energy, whether they realize it or not. If you are finding it difficult to let go of a relationship that has ended or if you keep thinking about a certain person or event (such as a trauma or an argument), those are signs that could indicate the presence of cords that are keeping you attached to the person or situation. If you feel unlike yourself or low-energy in general and that isn't your usual state, you may have picked up some energy that doesn't belong to you that needs to be cleared. To do this ritual, it isn't necessary that you know who or what you are connected to; you may simply know or sense that this needs to be done.

To begin, ground (see appendix A for a full grounding meditation) and cast a protective circle (see appendix B), then call on your spiritual team for assistance and protection. You may wish to work with Archangel Michael for this cord-cutting ritual and any other high-vibrational allies you prefer. Place your significator card in front of the white candle, and place the black tourmaline on top of the card.

Meditate and focus first on your breath, then on your body. With your eyes closed, do an energetic scan of your body from head to toe and feel where there are any areas of pain, discomfort, or other sensations that are calling for your attention. Ask your allies to show you where cords need to be cleared. You may receive this information via memories or mental images of a person or situation, through physical sensations, or through other means. You may simply sense that an area of your body needs healing and love.

Light the candle with the intention that it brings you healing and restoration. Call on your allies and ask that they sever the connections completely and clear, release, and transmute all energies that do not serve your highest good. You can ask them to sever your connection with specific people, energies, or situations. Pass the black kyanite several times over any areas where the energy is being cleared; you can pass it through your entire energy field from head to toe if you feel you need to.

Sit in meditation and visualize all energies being transmuted and dissolved as the light from the candle moves over you and your allies bring you healing on all levels. During this process, visualize cords being removed and those empty spaces being filled with healing golden-white light. If you notice other cords or energies that need clearing, repeat the process. When it is done, see the flame of the candle surrounding you in golden-white light that heals, restores, and protects you. Ask your allies to seal a sphere of protection around you that allows in only what is for your highest good. You can also set the intention that you will work only with high-vibrational energies and that these are the only energies that are allowed around you. When you are ready, ground your energy and close the circle.

Both before and following this ritual, you may find it beneficial to take a bath with epsom salts or sea salt dissolved in the water. You can add any herbs to this cleansing bath as you feel guided. This is a ritual you can come back to again and again, as you feel the need. Following especially intense relationships or situations, you may find that different cords come up at different times as you are ready to clear them, heal, and move on.

A Healing Ritual

Work with the elements and your high-vibrational allies to bring you healing on every level. Best performed on a Sunday, Monday, or Thursday during the waxing or full moon.

What You Need:

Epsom salts

Lavender essential oil or lavender flowers (for purification and tranquility)

Sweetgrass or palo santo for smudging

Amethyst, clear quartz, and/or selenite, cleansed and charged (see page 45)
Sandalwood and/or frankincense incense or resin
One white or pink candle
Chalice or glass filled with water

Before beginning this ritual, it is recommended to first perform the above ritual to cut any cords of attachment to energies, situations, or people that are causing an energy drain. Above all, use your judgment. You may have been on the healing journey for a while and do not feel the need to clear any cords at the moment; trust yourself.

The wide variety of crystals that are available for healing may reward your further research, as many have specific attributes that can assist you depending on where you need a boost. If you feel drawn to a certain crystal, it is meant for you; trust your intuition to let you know what you need. Quartz is a magnificent master healer that also brings clarity and is an ally for manifesting and focusing your intentions. Selenite is a powerful, high-vibrational crystal that offers protection and cleansing.

Set up your workspace, then prepare a hot bath and dissolve the epsom salts in the water. You can sprinkle lavender essential oil into the water or use lavender flowers, which will distill their essence in the hot water, allowing you to reap the benefits. Take as long as you like in the bath, relaxing fully and allowing all of your cares to shift out of your awareness and vibration as you release them into the water to dissolve and clear. As you soak, notice any unpleasant thoughts or memories that come up and acknowledge that these are surfacing to be cleared. Simply notice them, then release them with the intention to clear, release, and transmute them, knowing that they are no longer a part of you. You can set the intention that you retain any wisdom or information from them and release the rest. Although you may remember them, they no longer have any bearing on you and are not part of your vibration anymore.

Feel into gratitude for the space you are in and thank your allies for their love and support. When you are ready, dry off completely. You can dress in ceremonial clothing or in a certain color you feel drawn to (white is a good color for healing), but it isn't necessary for you to wear anything special. Smudge yourself and your space with the sweetgrass or palo santo. Cast a protective circle and call the quarters (see appendix B), then call in your high-vibrational allies.

Face north and hold the crystals you are using as you say:

In the north, I call upon the element of earth to assist me in healing on every level, in body, mind, and spirit.

Place the crystals in the north, sending them gratitude for their support.
Place the incense in the east and light it, then say:

In the east, I call upon the element of air to assist me in healing on every level, in body, mind, and spirit.

Place the candle in the south and light it, then say:

In the south, I call upon the element of fire to assist me in healing on every level, in body, mind, and spirit.

Face west holding the water and infuse it with the vibrations of healing, keeping your focus on receiving the healing. This will imprint the water with your intention. Then say:

In the west, I call upon the element of water to assist me in healing on every level, in body, mind, and spirit.

Drink the water and place its vessel in the west.
Hold the crystals and visualize the circle filling with white light that also surrounds and fills you completely. With your eyes closed, scan your energy field and see where any energy is that needs to be cleared; you may see energy that is clearing as black specks or some other shape that will usually be dark in color. See it dissolving in golden light and set the intention that it is cleared, released, and transmuted. Continue this visualization until your field is completely clear. Release the energy, ground (see appendix A for a full grounding meditation), release the quarters, thank your allies, and close the circle.

An Energetic and Auric Clearing

Align your chakras and clear negative energies and thoughtforms. Best performed on a Saturday during the waning moon.

What You Need:
Obsidian, cleansed and charged (see page 45)
Selenite

Begin by casting a protective circle (see appendix B) and calling in your high-vibrational allies. Visualize a cord connecting you from your root chakra into the earth, and another cord connecting you from your crown chakra into the cosmos. You can hold the obsidian and selenite during this ritual or, if you are sitting cross-legged, you can place the crystals on your legs.

Send gratitude to the earth for all it provides and draw the golden earth light through the cord and into your root chakra; visualize it moving up from your root to your sacral chakra, then into your solar plexus, heart chakra, throat chakra, third eye, and crown chakra. As you are drawing the light upward, notice if it feels like it pauses at a certain chakra. If this happens, allow the light to work on the chakra for as long as it needs to before visually moving it upward; the light may be restoring your chakra to balance or alignment, or energizing it. You may or may not feel the energy of the light moving through your chakras at first, but with practice, you may be able to feel or sense it. As you are doing this, ask that the golden light aligns your chakras and brings them into perfect balance, perfect harmony, and perfect connection, all for your highest good, connecting them as they are meant to be connected.

Then direct your attention upward and ask the cosmic, universal, divine white light to enter you through your crown chakra. Visualize this happening as the light moves down through each chakra, from crown to root. Again, try not to force the light if it seems to rest in a certain chakra, as that area may need extra support at this time. Simply sense when the light is ready to continue and visualize it moving it down until it reaches your root chakra. Intend that the white light blends harmoniously with the golden earth light, bringing your chakras into perfect alignment, balance, and harmony, connecting them as they are meant to be connected.

When you are ready, send out the intention that all harmful and negative energies, thoughtforms, and everything that does not serve your highest good is shifted out of your vibration. You may feel this happening as the energies release. Then set the intention that everything you clear and release is transmuted; this ensures it is healed and does not linger, return, or go elsewhere in the world to affect others.

Continue with this process and be specific. For example, you could send out the intention that all energies hindering your progress or all energies that are blocking you from receiving energetic upgrades are shifted and cleared. You can always ask your high-vibrational allies to assist you with shifting out these energies and in helping you to know what needs to clear out of your field. Sometimes, especially when we are beginning the healing journey, we don't always know what needs to be cleared or what is holding us back.

When you state each aspect individually, focusing on one at a time, it allows for a more powerful shift to take place. For example, you could first clear out energies of hurtful words that have been spoken against you and wait for those energies to shift and transmute, then release the energies of mistrust, then clear out energies of confusion, and so on. Allow each to resolve before moving on to the next intention. Allow these intentions to occur to you naturally, flowing with what needs to be shifted and cleared out of your field and your vibration. Continue doing this until you feel clear.

Then bring in the energies you do want, welcoming them to you by name. Always be sure to first set the intention that only high-vibrational energies are allowed around you, and that you will only work with high-vibrational energies. You can say things like, *I welcome perfect clarity.* (Pause between each statement as you feel the energy you are bringing in.) *I welcome the knowing of my highest path and purpose. I welcome the knowing of the truth of who I am. I welcome my Source-aligned empowerment. I welcome the knowing of my sovereignty. I welcome freedom. I welcome my true strength, which comes from my Source. I welcome in my highest awareness.* The more you do this, the easier it becomes for you to get on a roll with your intentions, and what serves you comes to mind more readily. When you are done with this ritual, thank your allies, ground (see appendix A for a full grounding meditation), and close the circle.

You can perform this energetic shift anywhere—as you are driving, waiting for an appointment, or whenever you have some time alone with your thoughts. You do not necessarily need to be in circle to do it, or even begin with the chakra alignment. The simple intention of clearing and shifting certain aspects out of your field and replacing them with the desired energies is a powerful way to shift your vibration and clear out a lot of energetic dross. You will find that it gets easier with practice as you feel yourself becoming increasingly clear and shifting out more of the energies that are not serving you.

A House Clearing and Blessing Ritual

Use this two-part ritual to clear your space of the unwanted and bring in high-vibrational energies. The clearing is best performed on a Tuesday or Saturday during a waning moon. The blessing is best performed on a Monday, Tuesday, or Friday during a full moon.

What You Need:
For the clearing:

Smudging stick

Black tourmaline or obsidian, cleansed and charged (see page 45)

Dragon's blood incense

For the blessing:

Saltwater

Selenite

Frankincense resin

Censer (optional)

As you perform every step of this ritual, it is important that you are aware of your vibration. It is to your greatest benefit to raise your vibration before beginning to ensure that you are operating from a high-vibrational place of bringing in light, love, and positivity, rather than from a place of fear or counterproductive emotions such as anxiety or worry. This is an ideal ritual to perform when first moving into a new place, and it is a good idea to use it to refresh the energy periodically. You will also want to repeat this ritual after any unwanted energies have entered your home, for example, following unpleasant experiences.

Note that if you are banishing or clearing out unwanted energy, you will want to move counterclockwise as you recite the clearing mantra. To bring in positive energy, you should work your way around your home clockwise as you recite the blessing mantra.

The Clearing

Make sure all windows are open. Place black tourmaline or obsidian in the north, east, south, and west of your home. Light a stick of dragon's blood incense in each room. Call on your high-vibrational allies and ask them to facilitate the removal of energies and ensure this is handled in the highest way. Starting and ending at the main entrance of your home, work your way counterclockwise around the perimeter with the lit smudging stick as you recite the following in your mind while holding the strong intention of the words:

> *I command all harmful energies to leave and never return.*
> *I command all energies that are not of a high vibration to leave and never return.*
> *Only high-vibrational energies are welcome here.*
> *Only high-vibrational energies may remain.*

After you have made your way back to the entrance, place the smudging stick at the door on a plate and allow it to burn out on its own. Thank your allies for their assistance.

The Blessing

Depending on how much preparation work needs to be done, you may want to set aside anywhere from an entire weekend to several hours for this ritual. Before beginning, open all windows and clear any clutter that you will discard from every room, removing it from your home. If you are setting aside bags or boxes for donation, place them in your vehicle to drop off later or otherwise remove them from the area you will be energetically clearing. Take all discards out to the trash bin. Once this is done, physically clean each room, being very thorough; clean all objects in the room, wipe down walls and doors with saltwater, then sweep and vacuum. Even if your floors are clean, sweeping clears out stagnant energy.

Make sure all windows are open. Place selenite in the north, east, south, and west of your home. Then, starting and ending at the main entrance of your home, work your way clockwise around the perimeter of your home. Sprinkle saltwater as you recite the following in your mind while holding the strong intention of the words:

> *Highest-vibrational peace, light, and love*
> *And protection divine*
> *Fill and surround this home and property*
> *And protect the dear ones who dwell within*
> *High-vibrational energies and allies*
> *Bless this home and those who live here*
> *With grace, harmony, love, and peace*
> *With clarity, wisdom, and understanding*

High-vibrational energies and allies
Protect those who live here
For now and for all time
Only love and light and peace may enter here
Only love and light and peace may remain
This house and its inhabitants are blessed
Thank you, thank you, thank you.

Light the frankincense resin in the censer and repeat the above incantation as you again, slowly, move clockwise around the perimeter of your home, allowing the smoke to fill the space.

If your home is surrounded by land, it is recommended that you perform a blessing of the property as well (the methods for doing so are various; consult trusted practitioners or reputable resources for more on that process). It is also helpful to stay mindful of the feng shui in your home and assure that energy flows well in your spaces and walkways aren't blocked by furniture or other objects.

Chapter 13

The Blue Moon

A blue moon is the second full moon in a month or the third full moon in a season that has four full moons (a typical season has three), and seasonal blue moons make their appearance about every two and a half years. By definition, this moon hints at rarity, and so its uniqueness is amplified—even more so considering that it occurs as an extra moon, giving it twice the power of a regular full moon.

The tarot spreads included in this chapter explore what rare opportunities may be available to you and how to harness the energy around you to seize the moment.

The rituals in this chapter are for summoning once-in-a-lifetime opportunities and setting long-term goals to manifest big dreams.

Blue Moon Energy

The amplified power of blue moon energy is felt for about three days following the moon's peak intensity. You can use this energy to your advantage and plan ahead for rituals during this four-day span. Whether you are working on a large-scale manifestation like a career change or a long-distance move, or anything around expansion or major life changes, you can supercharge your rituals and spellwork during this time. (See appendix B for a full moon ritual around amplifying your intentions, which you can tailor to your desires.)

Spreads

Once in a Blue Moon

We've all heard the sayings "Hindsight is 20/20" and "If only I knew then what I know now." When we tune in to our inner wisdom and use tarot as a guide, we can gain awareness of the various facets of a situation and use the insight into what is becoming to mold and shape current and future events into an outcome that works to our greatest benefit.

As conscious cocreators, we have the unique ability to set our intentions for the way we want things to turn out instead of letting them happen *to* us. And as vibrationally aware beings, we have the added benefit of being able to feel into a situation in order to craft the best outcome, both for ourselves and to support others. Use this spread (see illustration 13-1) to tune in to the current energies and uncover what rare opportunities may be available to you, just waiting for you to reach out and grab them.

Suggested questions:

1. In what area of my life is there a rare opportunity?
2. What is the nature of the opportunity?
3. How can I make sure it doesn't pass me by?
4. How can I make the most of it?
5. What are my next steps?
6. What energies are supporting me now?

Illustration 13-1: Once in a Blue Moon

Carpe Diem!

While this is an all-purpose spread (see illustration 13-2) that can be used any time of year, regardless of the moon phase, it is especially helpful when you sense that something is in the air and your action may be required. This is a spread for those times when you are buzzing with excitement, thrilled with the feeling that change is certain and your senses are overwhelmed with the anticipation of knowing that things are in a state of flux and becoming.

Suggested questions:

1. What are the current energies at hand?
2. How can I take advantage of that energy?
3. What is changing for me?
4. What is becoming for me?
5. How will this impact me?
6. What action am I guided to take now?
7. What outcome will this have?
8. How can I reap the greatest benefit from these shifts?

Illustration 13-2: Carpe Diem!

Spells & Rituals
A Blue Moon Summoning

Use this ritual to draw rare opportunities to you. Best performed during a blue moon.

What You Need:
One silver or white candle
One gold or yellow candle
Tool for carving
Olive oil
Vervain (for prosperity)
Your significator card
Citrine, cleansed and charged (see page 45)
Quartz, cleansed and charged (see page 45)
Orange peel (for good luck)
Sandalwood incense
Pen and paper
Cauldron

Cleanse and purify all tools and ingredients, then ground (see appendix A for a full grounding meditation) and create a sacred space (see appendix B). With your carving tool, carve any magical symbols into the candles that correspond with your desired outcome (the rune *Fehu* or *Feoh* is one option; it symbolizes wealth and prosperity and looks like an upward-slanted letter F). Dress the candles by anointing them in olive oil and coating them in vervain. Place the candles in holders on either side of the cauldron, and place your significator in front of the cauldron, with the quartz and citrine on each side of your card. Call the quarters and welcome any high-vibrational allies you wish to work with.

Light the incense in honor of your allies and spend a moment in gratitude. Clearly and succinctly state your intention for this ritual and your desired outcome. Light the silver or white candle first and say:

Candle of the moon
Shine your light
Rare opportunities
Begin for me this night.

Light the gold or yellow candle and say:

Candle of the sun
Shine your light
Brilliant opportunities
Begin for me this night.

Place the orange peel in the cauldron. Write your desired outcome on the paper, then read it aloud, fold it up, and light it in the flame of either candle. Drop it into the cauldron on top of the orange peel and allow it to burn completely. Know that as it burns, your intentions are being delivered into the universe. When the paper has finished burning, place the lid on the cauldron. Leave the lid on (don't open it, as this will release the energies) and bury the peel and ashes in the ground under the moonlight on the third night following your ritual. Ground and close the circle.

Note that this spell acts as a catalyst to set the wheels in motion to bring what you desire to you. You shouldn't expect instant results, but do know that it is on its way. The stronger your trust (or better yet, your knowing) that it is coming, and the stronger your expectation, the more it will increase in momentum and manifest more quickly into the physical.

Blue Moon, Big Dreams

Create a talisman that will help you manifest your intentions. Best performed during a blue moon.

What You Need:
Quartz, cleansed and charged (see page 45)
Lavender (for happiness and longevity)
Green pine sprigs (for money and longevity)
A pinch of ground cinnamon (for success)
Pen and paper
Fabric square or pouch

This is a talisman that you can keep on your altar, in the corresponding gua of your home (see appendix C), or in any place that is meaningful to you. Choose the color of the ink and the fabric square or pouch based on the color correspondence that aligns with your intentions (see the correspondences chart in the introduction). If you are sewing your own pouch, choose a ribbon in a color that supports your intentions, and stitch the pouch before beginning, or you can simply bunch the fabric together and tie it around with the ribbon at the appropriate point in the ritual. As always, make sure everything is cleansed and purified beforehand, then gather your supplies and create a sacred space around you (see appendix B).

This is ideally performed in the light of the moon, either outside, on a porch, or by a window so you and your creation can soak in the luminance. Take a moment to sit with your intention and get really clear on the outcome you desire. See it, feel it, live it, breathe it, be it. Because seasonal blue moons make their appearance rarely, think in terms of major plans and life-changing goals. The energy of this ritual will carry through from this blue moon to the next, so expect it to take at least that long to fully manifest. Watch for steps toward your goal falling into place along the way, and be ready for any guidance.

With the light of the moon shining on the paper, write your intention in clear, direct wording. Holding the paper in the moonlight, say:

Blue moon light
Rare and bright
Bring forth the intention
I set out this night.

Fold the paper and place it in the pouch, and add the other ingredients, holding them up to the moonlight before adding them. Cinch the top and tie the ribbon around three times, knotting it once each time. For every knot you tie, say *It is done.* Hold the pouch up to the moonlight, letting the light infuse it. Leave it in a place—preferably indoors near your sacred space or altar or in the appropriate feng shui gua (see appendix C)—where it will soak up the moonlight overnight, on the night you create it and for the three nights following.

Let your intuition guide you as to where you should keep this talisman. You can re-infuse it with your intention on every full moon if you like, up until the next blue moon, simply by holding it and meditating on your desired outcome, and allowing it to soak in the light of the full moon overnight. Take note of any guidance or action steps that come to mind during these meditations, and at any other time. Move forward in the knowing that your intention is becoming, as you have released it to the universe, and the way will be shown to you.

CONCLUSION

It is my hope that you find in tarot all the depth and fascination it has to offer, and that you tap into its strengths as a sacred tool. Tarot is a versatile medium and even more so in the glimmer of the full moon's light. When we use this many-layered and much-loved oracle in conjunction with our own spiritual practices and in concordance with the phases of the moon, we are tapping into the current of energy that flows around us and through us—the *chi* that informs our lives.

Whether you tune in to tarot as part of your healing journey or to seek guidance on everyday (and not so everyday) questions, as you continue working with the cards and develop a stronger connection to them, you will find it more natural to derive meaning from them that goes beyond the standard guidebook explanations. Those of you who have a long-standing relationship with tarot already understand this. When it comes to cartomancy, a bird is not just a bird, but a symbol of meaning; it interacts not only with the question and the querent, but with the other symbols on the card and the other cards in the reading.

May you find in tarot a means of gaining a greater awareness of yourself and the universe in which you live and clarity on your individual path and your unique soul's journey. Through this discovery, may you strengthen the light within so that you may send it out into the world. May you find in tarot a meaningful way of strengthening your connection with the divine and your relationship with your guides and higher self. Using tarot in conjunction with the energies of the moon can help you to manifest, to heal, to grow, and to gain increasingly deeper levels of clarity; it can help you to connect more powerfully to your intuition and better understand the world around you, as well as your own internal landscape which, like the phases of the moon and the tides of the ocean, is ever-shifting, always changing, and flows with the rhythms of the universe in an endless, eternal dance.

Appendix A

MEDITATIONS

A Grounding and Protection Meditation

This all-purpose grounding and protection meditation is powerful and I recommend starting every day with it. If you do not incorporate it into your daily practice, however, it is a good idea to do before beginning any spells, rituals, deep meditations, healing, or journey-work. It is written in the first person, and you may choose to repeat the words below aloud or to yourself. After you gain familiarity with it, you may want to adapt it to suit your preference.

Begin by sitting comfortably and entering a relaxed, meditative state. With your eyes closed, visualize each part of the meditation to further empower it.

The Meditation

I send a beam of light down from my core into the center of the earth. I send a beam of light up into the cosmos, connecting to the heavens and to the earth simultaneously. I greet you, dear Gaia, as I ground in earth. I send you my deep love and gratitude, Mother Earth. Thank you for all that you provide. Thank you for providing me and every being on this planet with nourishment, shelter, medicine, warmth, and wisdom. Thank you for your abundant beauty, which you give so freely and which nurtures and nourishes the soul. I am grateful to be in this body, on this planet, living this human experience with you, Gaia. Thank you for giving of yourself so freely and for supporting life on this planet.

I send you healing blessings, Gaia. May every square inch of this planet and the earth's atmosphere be completely healed, renewed, restored, replenished, rejuvenated, purified, uplifted, and made whole once again. Let there be perfect balance where balance is meant to be. Let there be overflowing abundance where abundance is meant to be. Let every species that is meant to be on this planet be on this planet in healthy numbers.

(Sit in gratitude and ask Gaia for any wisdom or messages she may have for you. Take a few moments to simply receive.)

I draw the golden earth light into me—into my root chakra, sacral chakra, solar plexus, heart chakra, throat chakra, third eye, and crown chakra. The golden earth light fills me: my head and brain, throat and neck, shoulders, arms and hands, back, chest, torso, internal organs, legs, ankles, feet, and toes. The golden earth light fills me, encompasses me, and surrounds me on every layer and level of my being and existence, across all times, dimensions, space, and realities (repeat this sentence three times as you visualize the light surrounding you, filling you, and expanding outward). The golden earth light heals me and aligns my chakras, bringing them into perfect balance and harmony, connecting them perfectly, exactly as they are meant to be connected. The golden earth light clears and transmutes all blockages, everything that is ready to be released, all energy that is not my own, and everything that is not in alignment with my highest good. In this protective sphere of golden light, only high-vibrational energies may be, only high-vibrational energies may enter (say this three times).

I focus my attention up into the cosmos and tap into the cosmic, universal, divine white light. I draw the cosmic, universal, divine white light down into me—into my crown chakra, third eye, throat chakra, heart chakra, solar plexus, sacral chakra, and root chakra. The white light gently merges and mingles with the golden earth light, creating a perfect, harmonious balance of golden-white light. The golden-white light fills me, surrounds me, and encompasses me on every layer and level of my being and existence, across all times, dimensions, space, and realities (say this sentence three times). The golden-white light fills me—my head and brain, throat and neck, shoulders, arms and hands, back, chest, torso, internal organs, legs, ankles, feet, and toes. The golden-white light aligns my chakras, bringing them into perfect balance, perfect harmony, perfect clarity, and perfect alignment, connecting them as they are meant to be connected. The golden-white light heals me on every layer and level of my being and existence, across all times, dimensions, space, and realities. In this protective sphere of golden-white light, only high-vibrational energies may enter, only high-vibrational energies may be (repeat this sentence three times).

I am blessed, I am protected, I am divinely guided. Thank you, Source; thank you, God, Goddess, and all that is; thank you, universe; thank you, One; thank you, All; thank you, high-vibrational allies, gods and goddesses, star beings, and ascended masters who are supporting me on my journey; thank you, guides; thank you, archangels and angels; thank you, inner being; thank you, high-vibrational divine allies, elements and elementals; thank you to the guardians of the earth and all high-vibrational beings who are supporting me on my journey. Thank you, thank you, thank you. Blessed be. (You can give gratitude and close however you like, then spend a moment setting your intentions for the day ahead.)

Once you close, you may choose to sit and meditate for a while, holding the intention of receiving any messages that are available to you from your allies.

An Alternate Grounding and Protection Meditation

This version is similar to the above meditation, but uses a different method of bringing in the cosmic, universal, divine white light and golden earth light. Both methods are effective but each uses a different approach, so it is recommended to try both and determine which one resonates with you. You may find that one or the other is more powerful for you depending on your energy and needs at the time, so your preference may be to alternate between them.

The Meditation

Sit comfortably and tune in to your energy. Send a cord into the earth with the intention of connecting with the earth energy then send a cord connecting you from your crown chakra into the cosmos so that you are connected to the heavens and the earth simultaneously. Say:

The golden earth light and the cosmic, universal, divine white light enter into me, merging and mingling to create a perfect, harmonious balance of golden-white light that fills me, surrounds me, and encompasses me on every layer and level of my being and existence, across all times, dimensions, space, and realities. (Say twice as you visualize this happening:) *The golden white light fills me, surrounds me, and encompasses me on every layer and level of my being and existence, across all times, dimensions, space, and realities.*

As you say the above, envision the earth light and the cosmic white light entering into you from above and below, merging within you, clearing, aligning, and connecting your chakras, and expanding to create a powerful sphere of protection around you that encompasses your entire aura. If you are sensitive to energy, you may feel the light from above and below coming together, filling you, and expanding to surround you.

You may choose to give thanks to Gaia and to your allies, ask them for their guidance, support, and protection as you wish, set your intentions for the day ahead, then close in gratitude.

Appendix B

AMPLIFYING YOUR INTENTIONS: A FULL MOON RITUAL

The full moon's intense energy makes it a powerful time to amplify your intentions. Setting intentions during the new moon and performing a ritual during the full moon helps bring your manifestations into culmination in a powerful way. Performing the ritual outside under the full moon is ideal, or you can do this near a window indoors if you don't have a private space outside where you can practice.

Begin by grounding and cleansing yourself with a ritual bath or with sage. Gather candles, crystals, incense, offerings such as flowers and wine or juice, something to write with, saltwater, an athame, a chalice, and any other tools you wish to use. Clear the energy in the space where you will be working with sage, cedar, or ethically sourced palo santo, and cleanse and purify any tools you will be working with (see page 45). You may want to create a circle of salt around you, especially if you are outdoors; make sure it is unbroken until you close the circle and complete the ritual.

Cast a circle and call the quarters. If you don't already have a preferred way of doing this, you can use the following. Cast the circle by saying the below three times as you turn clockwise, repeating once per rotation: *I cast this circle to create a sacred space. Only high-vibrational energies may enter this space.*

On the third iteration, say: *The circle is now cast. So mote it be. Blessed be.*

Quarter calls:

(Face north) Hail to the guardians of the watchtowers of the north. I call upon the element of earth. Hail, honor, and welcome to the circle.

(Face east) Hail to the guardians of the watchtowers of the east. I call upon the element of air. Hail, honor, and welcome to the circle.

(Face south) Hail to the guardians of the watchtowers of the south. I call upon the element of fire. Hail, honor, and welcome to the circle.

(Face west) Hail to the guardians of the watchtowers of the west. I call upon the element of water. Hail, honor, and welcome to the circle.

Call in any divine beings and high-vibrational allies you wish to work with, then thank and honor those you have summoned and present the offerings to them. Clearly state your intention and thank your allies for assisting you with its manifestation.

You may choose to employ chanting, drumming, and/or meditation as ways to raise the energy, connect with the energies that are supporting you, and reach an altered state from which you can do any journeywork or visualization. Write down your manifestation (you can use one you seeded on the new moon) as though it is already done, then bury it or burn it to release its energy into the universe.

Use the following chant to call on the powers of the elements:

(Face north) By the power of earth my will is made manifest on this physical plane and it is amplified.

(Face east) By the power of air my will is breathed into the universe around me and flows its energy to me now. Amplify!

(Face south) By the power of fire my will is ignited and amplified.

(Face west) By the power of water my will flows my manifested intentions to me now. Amplify!

(Face north) It is done, it is done, it is done. Blessed be.

Focus your energy and intentions and send them up into the universe. Give thanks and pour the wine or juice (if you are using it) onto the earth, thanking and releasing any beings you have called to the circle. Ground your energy. Release the quarters, then close the circle. You can use the following to close:

Turn counterclockwise as you close the quarters:

(Face west) To the west, I thank and release the element of water and the water guardian. Thank you for attending this circle.

(Face south) To the south, I thank and release the element of fire and the fire guardian. Thank you for attending this circle.

(Face east) To the east, I thank and release the element of air and the air guardian. Thank you for attending this circle.

(Face north) To the north, I thank and release the element of earth and the earth guardian. Thank you for attending this circle.

Close the circle by turning three times counterclockwise, saying the following with each rotation: *The circle is open but never broken. Merry meet and merry part and merry meet again.*

Appendix C

FENG SHUI BA GUAS

Understanding the energies that correspond with the various sectors, or *ba guas*, of your home is helpful when you want to support and energize a certain area of your life. To boost your finances, for example, you can set up coins and decorations that make you feel prosperous in the northwestern-most area of your home, the wealth *gua*. The chart on the next page can help you determine where to place vision boards, talismans, and other items you create with the intention of drawing a particular energy to that sector.

You can also use the chart for a tarot spread. Before drawing each card, simply hold the intention that the card you'll pull will reveal your current state of alignment with each *ba gua*. Once you have an idea of where you stand in each area of your life, you can then work toward strengthening any sectors that could use more support. You may also wish to draw a card for each *ba gua* that reveals any guidance that can help you strengthen those areas of your life.

West	North			East
	Finances	Achievement	Love	
	Family	Self	Children	
	Knowledge	Career	Community	
	South			

BIBLIOGRAPHY

Books

Ahlquist, Diane. 2017. *Moon Magic.* Avon, MA: Adams Media.

———. 2002. *Moon Spells.* Avon, MA: Adams Media.

———. 2020. *The Moon and You.* Avon, MA: Adams Media.

Alexander, Skye. 2017. *The Modern Witchcraft Book of Tarot: Your Complete Guide to Understanding the Tarot.* Avon, MA: Adams Media.

Cunningham, Scott. 2019. *Cunningham's Encyclopedia of Magical Herbs.* 2nd ed. Woodbury, MN: Llewellyn Publications.

Darcey, Cheralyn. 2018. *The Book of Herb Spells.* Summer Hill, Australia: Rockpool Publishing.

Dugan, Ellen. 2009. *Book of Witchery: Spells, Charms & Correspondences for Every Day of the Week.* Woodbury, MN: Llewellyn Publications.

Goddard, Neville. 2012. *The Neville Goddard Lectures, Volume 2.* Altenmünster, Germany: Jazzybee Verlag.

Gray, Eden. 1971. *Mastering the Tarot.* New York: Signet.

Greer, John Michael. 2003. *The New Encyclopedia of the Occult.* St. Paul: Llewellyn Publications.

Hicks, Esther, and Jerry Hicks. 2004. *Ask and It Is Given.* New York: Hay House.

Machamer, Peter, ed. 1998. *The Cambridge Companion to Galileo.* Cambridge, UK: Cambridge University Press.

Penczak, Christopher. 2004. *The Outer Temple of Witchcraft: Circles, Spells, and Rituals.* Woodbury, MN: Llewellyn Publications.

Toynbee, Emma. 2018. *Positively Tarot: A Modern Guide to a Mindful Life.* New York: Harper Design.

Wen, Benebell. 2015. *Holistic Tarot.* Berkeley: North Atlantic Books.

Online Resources

American Indian Alaska Native Tourism Association. 2019, 2020. "Native American Moon Names." Accessed December 2019 and March 2020. https://www.aianta.org /native-american-moon-names.

Excellence Reporter. 2019. "Nikola Tesla: On the Wisdom and the Purpose of Life." Accessed May 1, 2021. https://excellencereporter.com/2019/06/10 /nikola-tesla-on-the-wisdom-and-the-purpose-of-life/.

Hartman, Tori. 2020. "What Every Tarot Reader Needs to Know About Oracle Cards." Accessed January 2020. Biddy Tarot. https://www.biddytarot.com /tarot-and-oracle-cards/.

The Old Farmer's Almanac. 2020. "Full Moon Names: Native American and Other Traditional Names for Full Moons." September 23, 2020. https://www.almanac.com /content/full-moon-names.

Powell, Alvin. 2018. "When Science Meets Mindfulness." *The Harvard Gazette*, April 9, 2018. https://news.harvard.edu/gazette/story/2018/04/harvard-researchers-study -how-mindfulness-may-change-the-brain-in-depressed-patients.

Sagan, Carl. 1980. *The Cosmos.* Episode 1, "The Shores of the Cosmic Ocean." Aired September 28, 1980, on PBS. https://www.youtube.com/watch?v=FT_nzxtgXEw.

Sonnino, Elena. 2018. "7 Ways to Bring Your Intentions to Life." The Chopra Center. Last updated February 1, 2018. https://chopra.com /articles/7-ways-to-bring-your-intentions-to-life.

Zimecki, Michał. 2006. "The Lunar Cycle: Effects on Human and Animal Behavior and Physiology." Postępy Higieny i Medycyny Doświadczalnej. Last updated January 6, 2006. http://www.phmd.pl/api/files/view/1953.pdf.

Index

A

abundance, 10, 12, 13, 16, 20, 37, 40, 46, 47, 61, 62, 65, 87, 100, 101, 131, 133, 137, 138, 142, 156, 172, 187, 190, 222

alignment, 33, 34, 36, 65, 71, 74, 82, 85, 104, 125, 142, 150, 160, 201, 206, 207, 222, 223, 229

archetypes, 162, 178, 196

aura, 37, 49, 50, 65, 224

automatic writing, 61, 186

B

balance, 8, 10, 13, 43, 74, 84, 127, 145, 159, 160, 206, 222–224

banishment, 20

beauty, 12, 13, 15, 33, 87–89, 99, 100, 109, 123, 222

blessing, 5, 12, 148, 172, 193, 208–210, 222

blocks, 36, 72, 94, 113, 133, 138, 142, 143, 159, 172, 177, 183

C

career, 5, 8, 15, 20, 23, 26, 38, 40, 94, 107, 165, 177, 178, 182, 184, 185, 187, 188, 212, 230

D

E

F

G

S

T

To Write to the Author

If you wish to contact the author or would like more information about this book, please write to the author in care of Llewellyn Worldwide Ltd. and we will forward your request. Both the author and publisher appreciate hearing from you and learning of your enjoyment of this book and how it has helped you. Llewellyn Worldwide Ltd. cannot guarantee that every letter written to the author can be answered, but all will be forwarded. Please write to:

Victoria Constantino
℅ Llewellyn Worldwide
2143 Wooddale Drive
Woodbury, MN 55125-2989

Please enclose a self-addressed stamped envelope for reply,
or $1.00 to cover costs. If outside the U.S.A., enclose
an international postal reply coupon.

Many of Llewellyn's authors have websites with
additional information and resources.
For more information, please visit our website at
http://www.llewellyn.com

Notes

_____

_____

_____

_____

_____

_____

_____

_____

_____

_____

_____

_____

Notes

_____

_____

_____

_____

_____

_____

_____

_____

_____

_____

_____

_____

Notes

_____

_____

_____

_____

_____

_____

_____

_____

_____

_____

_____

_____

Notes

_____